DATE DUE

In Quest of Community

AMERICAN CULTURAL HISTORY SERIES

Editors:

Loren Baritz, University of Rochester

William R. Taylor, State University of New York, Stony Brook

Writers and Partisans:

A HISTORY OF LITERARY RADICALISM IN AMERICA,
James Burkhart Gilbert

In Quest of Community:

SOCIAL PHILOSOPHY IN THE UNITED STATES, 1860–1920
R. Jackson Wilson

In Quest of Community:

Social Philosophy in the United States, 1860-1920

R. JACKSON WILSON

JOHN WILEY AND SONS, INC.
New York • London • Sydney • Toronto

Library of Congress Catalog Card Number: 68-30924
SBN 471 94960 4
Printed in the United States of America

For Carl Bogholt,
Teacher

Acknowledgments

This book was influenced by three others. It is more accurate to say that it grew out of three others: Stanley Elkins' *Slavery*, R. W. B. Lewis' *The American Adam*, and William R. Taylor's *Cavalier and Yankee*. I am grateful to Mr. Elkins and Mr. Taylor for being willing to read the manuscript and to offer me not only criticism but encouragement. A fourth book, Robert Wiebe's *The Search for Order*, was published after I had completed my work. I have had from it and from its author a generous portion of confirmation and some of the nerve it takes to put my own book into print. It is unnecessary to add that I do not want to implicate any of these men in my mistakes and shortcomings.

Loren Baritz's careful and firm criticism has been very valuable, though both he and I wish that more of his recommendations had been executed. The number of other people who have read and criticized all or part of the book is almost embarrassingly large. I can only list them as a gesture in the direction of gratitude: David Allmendinger, Paul Bourke, Neil Coughlan, John Culver, Charles Forcey, John M. Gaus, John Livingstone, Eric McKitrick, Stephen Nissenbaum, Charles Strickland, and Allen Weinstein. I should also like to thank the fellow members of my seminars at the University of Wisconsin and my little handful of graduate students at the University of Arizona.

I owe debts to the Woodrow Wilson Fellowship Foundation, the University of Wisconsin and the University of Arizona for financial assistance.

There is no way to thank Merle Curti, my major professor and friend, for the things he has done. I hope that the publication of this book during the year of his retirement will serve as a small tribute to him.

My deepest obligation, in every way possible, is to my wife Carolyn.

R. JACKSON WILSON

Northampton, Massachusetts
May 22, 1968

Contents

In Quest of Community

Chapter 1

The Plight of the Transcendent Individual

The history of ideas in America had one of is beginnings in an eloquent assertion of the ideal of community. In 1630, on board the ship *Arbella* bound for New England, John Winthrop pleaded with his company of migrants to be "knit together in this work as one man." Winthrop was painfully conscious of the threats to social coherence that he and the settlers would meet in the New World. It was never too early for preventive defense, and the obvious line of defense lay in Winthrop's heritage of Christian organicism:

> We must delight in each other, make each other's condition our own, rejoice together, mourn together, always having before our eyes our Communion and Community in the work, our Community as members of the same body.[1]

Winthrop's lecture was an uncannily accurate prediction of the social values that were to meet the gravest challenges in America —stability and unity. He spoke in echo of a cultural situation that the *Arbella* was leaving behind, both in space and in time, and much of American history during the following two centuries amounted to a developing and increasingly conscious refusal to live by any ideal of community.

Winthrop's lecture was on "charity," or the social debts godly men owed one another. He distinguished two kinds of circumstances, ordinary and extraordinary, which dictated, in turn, two

[1] John Winthrop, "A Model of Christian Charity," in Perry Miller and Thomas H. Johnson, eds., *The Puritans* (Rev. ed., two vols., New York, 1963), I, p. 198.

kinds of social "charity." In ordinary circumstances men owed each other the kinds of loyalties that emphasized inequality and hierarchy. But in extraordinary circumstances (and what could be more extraordinary than the migration?) men owed one another an abrogation of self, status, and possession, a sacrifice of the private to the common weal. Winthrop's notion of the extraordinary was couched, in his letters and other writings, in the conventions of Old Testament history, but his perception of the temptations and dangers of the new continent was already modern and even American. For one thing, the very availability of the new land could not help but impress and unsettle the mind of an English squire of the seventeenth century. It was some time before the available meadows and hillsides could be grouped and conceptualized under the heads of "frontier" and "West." But Winthrop already knew (and soon learned even better) the plain fact that new land subverts order. In the second place the settlers were, by the standards to which Winthrop was accustomed, heterogeneous and would soon become more so. No significant passage of time was required before it became an American tautology that heterogeneity breeds liberty. Finally, and most important, Winthrop and his fellow-Puritans had been challenging institutional continuity and order for a generation and more. The gravest problem he faced in 1630 and after was the problem of having achieved local success, the problem of creating and maintaining new restraints on the deeds and thoughts of men. Before a decade had passed in New England, Winthrop encountered the concrete outcomes of local victory over Church and Crown. The encounters became almost the classic model of experience in America—liberation from "tyranny," followed hard and fast by the self-conscious creation of new, "free," but inevitably coercive means of stability and cohesion, followed again by new challenges in the name of liberty redefined.

These processes, as they pushed in an amplified way into the nineteenth century, created a society whose dynamic was centrifugal and whose public ideology was individualism. There were pockets of resistance, as there were bound to be. Old Federalists, Old Puritans and Old Planters groused in their different ways about new men and new ways, but by the 1830s, in economic theory, in political thought, even in theology, individualism of one kind or another had won the intellectual day. The victory was the outcome of dozens of decisions by poets, ministers, public men, and other would-be intellectuals, decisions to celebrate rather than lament the new man and his new nation. From Winthrop's day to Ralph Waldo Emerson's, every man of wit and learning in America made a choice (usually a covert and even preconscious choice) between what was old and supposedly cohesive and what was new and supposedly liberating. The plainest fact about American letters up to the 1830s is that most of the talent that got any kind of use and expression opted for the liberation of mind, vote, soul, and pocketbook from churches, from theologies, from Crown, and every legislative entailment, from John Calvin, from mortmain and vested interest. The process was not simple and it was not glacially regular; there were vivid exceptions and shadings aplenty. But the process nevertheless did occur, and it comes as close as anything can to constituting the relative distinctiveness of men's experience in America.

One of the intellectual climaxes of this cultural process was Ralph Waldo Emerson's 1836 essay on *Nature*. *Nature* was a schema of conversion, stripped of the conventional vocabulary of Christianity, but claiming nevertheless to point a way toward a species of salvation. The first step in the schema was prescribed in the famous dictum, "To go into solitude, a man needs to retire as much from his chamber as from society." From this deceptively gentle opening Emerson went on to argue, without the compromises so typical of most of his writing, that virtue was accessible only to the individual who stepped outside the kinds of associations suggested by "chamber" and "society." The point was made clearly in a play on words on the idea of ownership:

> The charming landscape I saw this morning is indubitably made up of some twenty or thirty farms. Miller owns this field, Locke that, and Manning the woodland beyond. But none of them owns the landscape. There is a property in the horizon which no man has but he whose eye can integrate all the parts, that is, the poet.

The point of the conceit was radical. Emerson came very close, for a moment, to a final rejection of the foundations of society as he knew them: the possession of property functioned as an ugly obstacle to the direct possession of Nature—that is, in more conventional terms, to salvation.[2]

The radicalism of Emerson's argument was softened by gentle language and by his skill at arguing by oblique suggestion instead of logic and evidence. But this does not at all alter the fact that the essay rejected the relationship that Emerson thought lay at the base of his society. To "retire" from a chamber hardly suggested revolution, but the intent of the essay was very radical indeed. What made the radicalism safe—and made it possible for Emerson to become a genteel institution in his own right after a time—was its civil inconsequence. The poet could repudiate the ownership of farms as a symbolic repudiation of all institutions and history without doing the least harm to society. The revolution was private; the poet was freed and enabled to luxuriate in the possession of Nature, which, in turn, remained an affair of no direct instrumental import. The radicalism was, in a loose sense, esthetic. Its outcome was a liberated sensibility and an immediate enjoyment of a reality more skew than opposed to the society left behind. The poet-hero rejecting society was a conventional figure in the literature of the nineteenth century, especially in the literature of Emerson's period in America, and such a poet-hero was subversive only by implication. The individualism was so radical it was functionally inconsequential.

This noninstrumental radicalism hinged, in *Nature* and in many of Emerson's other essays, on a paradox quite central to Emerson's theoretical individualism. Once the poet—Emerson seemed to mean any sensitive individual—retired from chamber and society and entered into an immediate relationship with Nature, an odd thing happened. The individual no sooner gained identity in isolation than he lost it. If the opening step in Emerson's conversion schema was the assertion of privacy and personality, the closing step was a total denial of individuality. The pivotal passage on the ownership of farms suggested this consummation. The poet, with his eye, "integrated" the landscape. This meant, in terms of the pun, that he "had" the "property" of the horizon. But whatever has all the properties of a thing *is* the thing. And this was precisely the fate of the poet: he *became* Nature. Here

[2] *The Complete Works of Ralph Waldo Emerson* (Centenary Edition, Twelve vols., Boston, 1903-1904), I, p. 8.

was the point of the most famous metaphor of the essay: "All mean egotism vanishes. I become a transparent eyeball; I am nothing; I see all." Throughout Emerson's work were scattered numerous discussions of the heightened use of a sense, usually some special experience for the eye. And, always, the heightened quality of sensory experience was connected with a heightened individuality. But the paradoxical outcome was the same in almost every case; heightened individually eventuated in no identity at all. Emerson began with a triumphant claim that only the individual in solitude could be a locus of genuine value. But once solitude was achieved, once society was cast off, individuality was obliterated. The individual articulated his privacy only as a step toward losing it in the "currents of Universal Being."[3]

In the construction of this paradoxical schema of salvation Emerson brought together three terms which nineteenth-century thinkers put to most serious and confusing use—individual, society, and cosmos. Obviously such categories have been fundamental at every point in the history of ideas. For the intellectual of the nineteenth century, especially in its first half, what was most important was not the meanings of any of the terms but the discovery of difficulties in their relations. Traditionally (though with some important exceptions) European and American thinkers had conceived of societies and individuals as concentric parts of a natural order. Especially in the eighteenth century, European and American, men's failures had been almost universally explained as failures to align themselves, both as individuals and societies, with a natural order of one kind or another. What was most nearly new about the Emersonian assertion and its dozens of echoes in American literature and philosophy was the unqualified claim that society was an obstacle to the alignment of the individual with cosmic order. John Winthrop, and everyone who either came with him or shared his assumptions, could think of society only as the inevitable temporal matrix in which men played out their parts in the cosmic drama. In *Nature* there was a clear assumption that societies were barriers, not vehicles, and that man, if he was ever to confront Spirit, had to do so historically and institutionally naked.

In *Nature* this relationship among the ideas of individual, soci-

---

[3] *Works*, I, p. 10.

ety, and cosmos was quite plain; the poet quit society to gain genuine individuality and then submerged that individuality in cosmos. What was not clear, and never became clear in Emerson's
writings, was the content of the three terms. Individual and cosmos, despite Emerson's attempts to give them concreteness in metaphor, were only abstractions. The "I" of the essay was so abstract
and empty it was, even in metaphor, "transparent," And cosmos,
or Nature, was only an affair of "essences unchanged." The transparent self merged easily into an existentially vacuous cosmos,
and the outcome was an end to personal identity. Society, on the
other hand, was so hopelessly concrete it fell short of being a
workable conception at all. Society, not only in this essay but in
most of Emerson's writing, was represented only as a list of particulars like "chamber," the ownership of occasional farms, the
"din and craft of the street." Emerson simply lacked usable and
satisfying concepts of society, and so society could not function
for him as a mediating term between man and Nature. Any notion
of society as mediation was dropped out of the analysis of experience, and man was lured into solitude in a state of social undress
to be summarily ravished of identity. The idea seemed new, and
it had, really, nothing to do with the formalities of Kant's categorical imperative. Emerson could only hope it made sense: "Thus
it seems to be true that the more exclusively idiosyncratic a man
is, the more general and infinite he is, which though it may not
be a very intelligible expression means I hope something intelligible."[4]

The paradox of *Nature* was the outcome of a decade of intellectual and vocational difficulty for Emerson. Ten years before
he wrote the essay he was very far from believing that society
was an obstacle to virtue, a barrier between man and Spirit. In
fact, in the mid-1820s Emerson was not ready to perceive a polarization of individual and society. In 1827, when he was still a
student at Harvard Divinity School, he jotted down a list of
seven "Peculiarities of the Present Age." The second item on his
list was: "It is said to be the age of the first person singular."
(Ten years later he would have omitted the words "said to be.")

[4] Entry of September 27, 1830, *The Journals and Miscellaneous Notebooks
of Ralph Waldo Emerson*, William H. Gilman et al., eds. (Cambridge,
1962-   , III, p. 199.

The seventh peculiarity was: "The disposition among men of associating themselves to promote any purpose." There were, he added in parentheses, "Millions of societies." The important thing about this student list is not the latent contradiction between the "first person singular" and "millions of societies." What is important is that in 1827 Emerson did not notice any problem; nothing in the list provoked any further comment or explanation. Emerson, who usually used any opportunity to pursue his journal entries, ignored this chance and the odd juxtaposition of individuality and association remained, for the time being, unexplored.[5]

This lapse, which would have been quite impossible a few years later, was possible in 1827 because Emerson himself was thoroughly committed to a form of "association," to an institutional role for himself that would have made the idea of "retiring" from chamber and society repugnant. In 1827 Emerson was an aspirant to the Unitarian ministry, and he approached his career in the most professional manner, carefully noting the ministerial appointments of his contemporaries, commenting on their professional styles, trying to read his vocational future in their lives. With this vocational commitment and ambition went a corresponding intellectual commitment to the value of "association" and "societies." One of Emerson's most striking sermon plans, written in 1827, was a discussion of the communal nature of the Christian life. "When we came up this morning to the house of God," he began, "did we come up in savage solitude, each from his lonely house, a congregation of hermits to whom society is unwelcome?" His answer to this potent question was reminiscent, in both style and intent, of John Winthrop's *Arbella* lecture. "We came up to the house of God in company," Emerson insisted:

> We have taken sweet counsel together. We do not live for ourselves, we do not rejoice, we do not weep alone. Our lives are bound up in others. Our blood beats in our breasts pulse for pulse with a true accord at the honor and the shame of a hundred other hearts to which God has united us in family or friendship.

In the 1820s Emerson conceived his own "priestly" role, as he called it, as that of father to a congregation considered as a familial company. This usable conception of society and of role within it meant, of course, that the polarities of *Nature* were not pres-

---

[5] Entry of c. January 30, 1827, *Journals,* III, pp. 70-71.

ent in anything like a developed form. If there was no need to retire into solitude, there was no need to think of the self as an abstraction. The identity of the self could be taken more or less for granted as a set of inherited definitions.[6]

Personal identity meant, to the young Emerson, a consciousness of locus in history and institutions, utterly opposed to the blankness of Nature. Emerson's sense of this kind of identity was confident. By 1836, of course, he had in mind a different kind of identity-in-isolation that erased the historical and institutional coordinates of personality, generalizing the individual abruptly into transparency. A concomitant of this, in *Nature*, was the rejection of history. "Our age is retrospective," he complained. "Why should we grope among the dry bones of the past, or put the living generation into masquerade out of its faded wardrobe?" But in 1827, the year he wrote out his sermon on the communal congregation, he felt very differently. History was "premiere in the cabinet," a phrase as stuffily conservative in tone as in intent. And he revelled in his own sure sense of the continuity of past and present. "I am in the pleasant land of my fathers," he wrote a Harvard classmate, "and of my sons and sons' sons peradventure." This confidence of historical continuity implied a similar awareness of locale at odds with the placelessness of Nature as he later was to conceive it. In 1827 when the possibility developed of a ministerial appointment in New York, Emerson refused it. "For myself," he reasoned, "I would rather be a doorkeeper at home than bishop to aliens."[7]

Emerson's perception of himself and his world in the 1820s was not, naturally, without serious doubts. There were points at which he sensed and even desired abstraction from Cambridge and Boston, from ancestry, and from his career. In his journals and letters a running dialogue developed in which the values of *Nature* emerged as a counterpoint to the themes of the ministry, locale, and history. The dialogue and the emergence of the ideal of transcendence were not, however, purely intellectual developments; Emerson's existential situation as a divinity student and a

[6] Sermon sketch, June, 1827, *Journals*, III, p. 91.
[7] *Nature*, *Works*, I, p. 3; Emerson to William Emerson, October 31, 1827, in *The Letters of Ralph Waldo Emerson*, Ralph L. Rusk, ed. (Six vols., New York, 1939), I, p. 218; Emerson to John Boynton Hill, June 19, 1823, *Ibid.*, p. 132; Emerson to William Emerson, January 6, 1827, *Ibid.*, p. 185.

Boston minister were an integral part of the polarization. The fortunes of his career were as important to the rhetorical rejection of chamber and society in *Nature* as any reading he did in Plato, Kant, or English and German Romantic literature. As long as the ministry was even marginally satisfying, the notions of *Nature* could not develop. When the ministry failed Emerson as a vocation (or, as he viewed it much of the time, when he failed the ministry) the rejections of chamber and society became a necessity. The church and the congregation were at the center of every conception of social community Emerson had as a young man. When he resigned his pulpit in 1832, he did not leave only a profession; he also relinquished the only social language he was ever to speak with any fluency. The enveloping, dissolving ideal of Nature, in the essay of 1836, was in its deepest reality a substitute for the congregation, a cure for the "savage solitude" that had seemed in 1827 to be the alternative to the congregation and the ministry.

Emerson's retirement from the ministry, like the poet's retirement from chamber and society, dramatically liberated him from history and institutions. But liberation from community also liberated Emerson, like his poet, from identity. The notion of Nature was the matrix for a new, merely potential, identity with the cosmos, a community within the Oversoul. Nature, in other words, was a metaphor for all potential forms of satisfactory integration of the individual into working wholes. *Nature,* then, was programmatic. It forecast that once the individual was set free from false involvements in chamber and society, fresh and genuine involvements would come to him. But *Nature* did not, as it could not in 1836, designate concretely any of the potential involvements. Nature was a metaphor whose object did not yet exist, a blueprint for a higher form of "association" whose details Emerson did not know. Some of his friends and followers attempted from time to time to experiment with what they thought were concrete arrangements for making Nature present and usable. Thoreau's stay at Walden Pond was one such experiment. The Brook Farm project of Emerson's Boston colleague, George Ripley, was another attempt to make Nature work, to make the metaphor ponderable and subject to manipulation. Brook Farm, especially in the early stages, attempted to recreate the congregation-as-family, justified no longer by the inherited associations of history but by the rhetoric of Nature. Emerson's difficulty was that, for various reasons, he was uncomfortable with any effort to make Nature instrumental. It remained for him a metaphor without object, an almost plaintive claim that spiritual forms of association must exist as antidotes to solitude, but at the same time an admission that their outlines were not visible.

The significance of Emerson's *Nature* was not that its ideas influenced this or that American intellectual, but that it epitomized a very widespread hope and dilemma. The ideal of the transcendent individual was by no means restricted to Emerson's circle or to Concord. Emerson captured in *Nature*, in a dramatic way, a vision of the radically free individual confronting reality, seeing clearly and directly into the sublime heart of the world, then ruthlessly testing the inheritance of the past and rejecting without qualm any that did not conform to liberated insight. This dramatized ideal was shared by dozens of abolitionists. In a less obvious form it was the most basic assumption of almost all academic philosophers in mid-nineteenth-century America. The transcendent individual was a key subject of inquiry for the best novelists of the period. Emerson lived at that disconcerting time in American history when a progressive atrophy in social institutions intersected with an almost violent expansion in territory, economy, and population. Part of the significance of *Nature* was that it captured some of this experience in a dramatic convention —the poet's rejection of history and confrontation with pure Nature. But the rejection and the confrontation created a new problem; what was to be done with the transcendent individual once the short, ecstatic drama was complete? How was the anti-historical, anti-institutional man to live in the world? Whoever examined or celebrated the liberated moral individual (and almost every American intellectual did so sooner or later) had to confront the difficulty.

No one, almost literally, was willing to go the whole way and accept an atomization of human experience into privacy and self-assertion. But this was the threat latent in the ideal of transcendence. The plainest need of Emerson's generation of American intellectuals was for working concepts of community which could replace the repudiated forms of chamber and society, positive laws, and family trees, all the inherited forms of identity and restraint. An answer like Thoreau's was plainly, even intentionally, unworkable. Brook Farm was just as eccentric and without Walden's saving irony. Nathaniel Hawthorne and Herman Melville could track the career of the transcendent individual only in tragedy. No one solved the problem, least of all Emerson. No one seemed able to discover usable communities in American life as it existed. The only alternatives seemed to be metaphor, eccentricity, or tragedy.

Nature was a temporary climax to a process of institutional withdrawal in Emerson's life. His career after 1836 reversed the process. Gradually, as he became a "sage," he resumed something of the sense of identity that had belonged to him in the 1820s. The simple fact of fame, the Lyceum tours, the endless Boston lectures, membership in the ultimately prestigious Thursday Club of Boston and in the American Association for the Advancement of Science, these and other engagements could demand only a recantation of *Nature*. After 1836 Emerson reverted, occasionally, to the rhetorical radicalism of *Nature*, but the effect of age and fame, on the whole, was to turn him into an advocate of whatever "civilized" man. Before he was sixty (not at all old as philosophers go) the process was complete.[8] In a lecture first delivered with the significant title "Civilization in a Pinch," written mostly in 1860, Emerson reversed all the major values of *Nature*. In the poem which introduced the lecture he used a log cabin at the edge of the wilderness as a symbol of culture, an outpost against the dark threats of the forest. By "Beethoven's notes . . . played with master's hand" inside the cabin, "The bear is kept at bay." Then, in a pair of lines that are remarkable when set against *Nature*, Emerson completely reevaluated the moral worth of a chamber and all it implied: "What in the desert was impossible, Within four walls is possible again." Emerson had swung

---

[8] As anyone who has spent much time with Emerson's writings, and especially with the journals, knows, it is not easy to generalize about Emerson's attitude toward even the most specific problems. There were times in the 1820s when Emerson forecast the language of his later individualism; in the mid-1830s, he sometimes referred to the social needs of men; and, in the 1840s and 1850s, there were reassertions of the radicalism of *Nature*. All any historian can do is to locate what seems to be the center of gravity of opinion, a problem particularly severe in Emerson's case.

back to the social insistences of the 1827 sermon on the congregation. Solitude, the bear, the forest were savage again, and
Beethoven-within-four-walls functioned as a symbol of human
possibilities. With this reversal went, inevitably, a retraction of
the poetic rejection of society. The senior Emerson, the member
of the Board of Overseers of Harvard, decided that "this banishment to the rocks and echoes no metaphysics can make right or
tolerable. . . . A man must be clothed with society."[9]

Merely changing his mind about the relative merits of society
and solitude did not solve the more serious problem of discovering concretely satisfying forms of society. Emerson's personal involvements might be adequate "clothing" for himself, but they
could hardly operate as philosophical alternatives to solitude.
Even after he became willing to set a high value on society, the
vocabulary Emerson used to discuss the problem was almost embarrassingly thin. As synonyms, not examples, for society, he
could use only such terms as "conversation," "soiree," "party,"
and, as a kind of ultimate confession of defeat, "cordials." As an
example of the isolation of genius from society, he pointed with
characteristic lameness to Dante's refusal of dinner invitations.
Emerson was still trapped by an acute lack of social imagination
and vocabulary. He was still unable, even after the reversals of
the 1840s and 1850s, to conceive of workable American communities. " 'Tis worse, and tragic," he had to conclude, "that no man
is fit for society who has fine traits. . . . But there is no remedy
that can reach the heart of the disease but either self-reliance . . .
or else a religion of love." Emerson was prepared, at this late
stage in his intellectual career, to admit the tragedy of a separation between individual and society, but he was ready with no
remedy. A "religion of love" was as merely potential and as abstract as the concept of Nature had been in 1836. The terms of
the problem had changed dramatically, but no solution was at
hand.[10]

Emerson's inability to think with any facility about social possibilities was most patently revealed by his response to the Civil
War. At last, in the war, he discovered what seemed for a time to
be a present and viable substitute for the ideal of the congrega-

9 "Civilization," *Works*, VII, p. 17; "Society and Solitude," *Ibid.*, p. 10.
10 "Society and Solitude," *Works*, VII, p. 7.

tion he had relinquished thirty years before. The hope of losing "mean egotism," the equivalent hope for a "religion of love," took functional shape. "War civilizes," he thought, "for it forces individuals and tribes to combine, and act with larger views, and under the best heads, and keeps the population together, producing the effect of cities; for camps are wandering cities."[11] The relief with which Emerson welcomed the war exemplified drastically the difficulty of discovering communities worthy of transcendent men. So long as Emerson still began with the ideal of the radically free individual, only something as apocalyptic and in its own way transcendent as war could be a satisfactory symbol of community.

Most of Emerson's generation of intellectuals (including many who sneered at the label "Transcendentalist") centered their views of the world on one variant or another of the transcendent individual. This meant, in turn, that they shared Emerson's problem. William Lloyd Garrison, for example, was as insistent as Emerson, though in a different way, on the ultimate reality of the free individual. Garrison was deeply affected by a sectarian version of individualism, religious perfectionism. Perfectionism, the stock in trade of revivalists like Charles Grandison Finney, was grounded in the notion that a man could become perfectly sanctified by a "second blessing," and, as a result, could gain a real identity with Christ. This ideal of perfection, which had a considerable number of adherents among clergymen and reformers like Garrison, employed an overtly Christian vocabulary. But the vocabulary described a self-determining, world-transcending individual recognizably similar to Emerson's poet-in-Nature. The perfectionism of Garrison and other reformers was, like Transcendentalism, insistently antinomian; both implied a thorough, even ruthless, criticism and repudiation of existing social institutions. The same logic that might send Bronson Alcott or Thoreau to jail forced Garrison to burn the Constitution, symbolically destroying the structure of society in America as an indispensable prelude to the creation of a community fit for moral man.[12]

---

[11] Quoted by Edward Emerson, in *Works*, VII, p. 356.
[12] On Garrison and perfectionism, see John L. Thomas, *The Liberator:*

Garrison's sometime friend and adviser, John Humphrey Noyes, surpassed even Garrison's faith in the morally liberated individual. Noyes believed that he had actually received the second blessing and was therefore perfected. The immediate outcome was what Noyes called a "Declaration of Independence" from the United States, a demand for the "overthrow" of all civil machinery. But the trajectory of racial individualism ran its course in Noyes to a conclusion in utopian communism. The ideal of the spiritually self-sufficient individual generated a need for a balancing antipode. Noyes' movement from the perfected individual to the Oneida community experiment had the same intellectual shape as the journey of Emerson's poet, out of society into symbolic solitude to blend personality in the larger whole of Spirit. Garrison's slogan, "No Union with Slaveholders," was an outcome of religious individualism, but it was also a recognition that existing, false forms of society must be broken as a step toward real community. Noyes, not sidetracked for long into the antislavery movement, simply worked out the intellectual drama to its conclusion and became a transcendental communist.[13]

Garrison and Noyes, in their radicalism, illustrate in an important way another paradox of the intellectual situation in America before the Civil War. A pledge of faith in the free individual was, after about 1830, the most characteristically American gesture any intellectual could make, but the gesture seemed to demand an un-American or even anti-American outcome. Measured by the transcendent standards of either antislavery perfectionism or Concord Transcendentalism, American life was not a satisfactory form of "association." So the most radical of individualists were also the most radical critics of America. As a result, they had to seek intimations of purer community outside the ordinary course of American experience. Emerson found tem-

William Lloyd Garrison, a Biography (Boston, 1963), pp. 223-235, and Walter M. Merrill, *Against Wind and Tide, A Biography of William Lloyd Garrison* (Cambridge, 1963), pp. 180-183. Emerson finally identified himself with Garrison (and with that other antinomian, Anne Hutchinson) in a Boston lecture of April 9, 1861. James Elliott Cabot, *A Memoir of Ralph Waldo Emerson* (Two vols., Boston, 1887), II, p. 779.
13 On Noyes, the best source is *The Religious Experiences of John Humphrey Noyes*, George Wallingford Noyes, ed. (New York, 1923), much more important to an understanding of Noyes's life than his classic *History of American Socialisms* (Philadelphia, 1870).

porary relief in war, Garrison in the contemplation of secession and the creation of a new nation in the North. Noyes and the founders of other "come-outer" communities resolved the perplexities of their individualism in schemes of "social reorganization." The extremity and the latent anti-Americanism of social solutions increased in rough proportion to the extremity of individualist premises. Most American thinkers perceived their national history as a progressive liberation of the individual, but this dominant note in their thought had its antithetical need for balancing social values. There was no American *ancien régime* with any substantial social potential, so the need for moral community found imaginative satisfaction elsewhere in time or space, in a colonial or non-American past, in Catholicism, in the South Seas, in Europe, and in utopian futures. The symbols of potential community were richly varied and sometimes contradictory, but they had one thing in common—they were out of joint with nineteenth-century America. Whenever community became a need and a value, it was symbolically located in something foreign, eccentric, or apocalyptic.

Thoreau told the story with characteristic precision in his account of a trip through Canada made between his stay at the Pond and the publication of *Walden*. At numerous points in "A Yankee in Canada," he insisted on the foreign quality of life, the contrasts with America; and, as a fundamental part of the contrast, he imputed to the French Canadians a social coherence and a sense of community that were missing in the Yankee. "If the Canadian wants energy, perchance he possesses those virtues, social and others, which the Yankee lacks, in which case he cannot be a poor man." Within this pointedly foreign context, Thoreau discovered the most suggestive symbol of community in the most un-American phenomenon—the drill of English regulars in Montreal, "one of the most interesting sights I saw in Canada." He was disgusted, for the spectacle ran directly counter to the values of *Walden;* the movement of the troops reminded him of a centipede. But there was a significant balancing element in the experience; the drill seemed at least to hint of social harmony. The soldiers moved their "hands," and perhaps even their "heads" in unison. "But if they could put their hands and heads and hearts and all together, such a cooperation and harmony would be the very end for which governments now exist in vain." *Walden,* like *Nature* or the antinomian assertions of perfectionism, was not a rejection of society as such, but only of society as it was actually available in America. The foreign setting, the unfamiliar drill of troops, focused Thoreau's imagination on the ideal of a good community of "all together."[14]

To secure the point, Thoreau recounted, in the same chapter of "A Yankee in Canada," his visit to the cathedral of Notre Dame in Montreal. The church had all the same qualifications of foreign unfamiliarity as the parade, and again Thoreau pointed overtly to the significance of the experience: "I saw that it was of great size and signified something." What the cathedral signified was the possibility that men might be bound together in institutions without being demoralized. The cathedral could hold ten thousand people at once and was open at all hours. But whether there were a few old women at worship or a great crowd, the church would still be "solitary." "I think," Thoreau concluded, "that I might go to church myself some Monday, if I lived in a city where there was such a one to go to." Then he compressed the whole schema of transcendence into a pair of sentences: "In Concord, to be sure, we do not need such. Our forests are such a church, far grander and more sacred." The substitution of Nature for institutions was precisely the same as Emerson's, and the identification of America with Nature and French Canada with institutions was clear. But there was an obvious wistfulness in Thoreau's response to the foreign, the communal, and the institutional, a wistfulness that threw a telling shadow on his explicitly confident, overtly American individualism.[15]

The same set of contrasting values, and the same wistfulness, occurred in Hawthorne's *The Marble Faun.* In the novel Haw-

14 "A Yankee in Canada," in *The Writings of Henry David Thoreau* (Twenty vols., Boston, 1906), V, pp. 16-17, 68.

15 "A Yankee in Canada," *Writings,* V, pp. 12-14. Emerson, during his European trip of 1832-1833 just after his resignation, fastened on the same kinds of values in Catholicism. "How beautiful to have the church always open," he wrote in Malta. It was "sublime" in St. Peter's when "All knelt as one man." In fact Emerson paid St. Peter's the highest compliment possible in the esthetic vocabulary of the day—it was the "sublime of the beautiful." *Journals,* IV, pp. 117. 157. But, in 1833, Emerson's insistent response to the lure of the cathedrals could only be the same as Thoreau's: "Here's for the plain old Adam." *Ibid.,* p. 84. Orestes Brownson and the significant handful of intellectuals who actually converted did so under the attraction of the same qualities of the Church that intrigued Emerson and Thoreau.

thorne constructed one of the most elaborate cases of transcendental privacy in American literature. Hilda, one of the heroines of the novel, was a "daughter of the Puritans," studying in Rome. Her relationship with the city, which was an emblem of all history and civilization, was one of almost total transcendence. She lived in a "tower," tending doves, virginal and completely out of touch with Rome. Her transcendence eventuated in a priggish inability to understand the sins of men, and a consequent failure to establish any real relationships with people who were nominally her friends. Finally, after witnessing a murder and feeling stained by her secret knowledge, Hilda began to visit St. Peter's. The confrontation was a fictional equivalent of Thoreau's visit to Notre Dame, and it produced the same kinds of responses.

First, Hawthorne made it clear that the cathedral and all it signified were corrupt and dangerous—much as Thoreau likened the British soldiers to a centipede. This much done, Hawthorne was free to let Hilda explore for a few pages the attractive qualities of Catholicism. Like Thoreau, Hawthorne pointed to the fact that the church was always open; whatever the hour, there were always penitents at hand. And, in the same way that Thoreau had made a point of the size of Notre Dame of Montreal, Hawthorne called St. Peter's the "World's Cathedral." There were confessionals for every language, so that "In this vast and hospitable cathedral, worthy to be the religious heart of the whole world, there was room for all nations; there was access to the Divine Grace for every Christian soul." Hilda enacted the potent ritual of confession and found relief from the private torments of conscience. But, like Thoreau, she drew back and returned to her tower and the doves. What counted for the novel, however, was not the impossible chance that she might actually be converted, but the dramatic encounter of American transcendence and Roman Catholicism. Hilda discovered a moral alternative to transcendent individualism, and Hawthorne made it clear that the alternative was also an alternative to America. The day before Hilda "confessed" she had contemplated going home to New England. After the experience in St. Peter's, she was "happy" again and prepared to stay longer in Rome.[16]

Emerson's conclusion that man must be clothed in society,

---

[16] *The Marble Faun, or the Romance of Monte Beni* (Washington Square Press edition, New York, 1958), pp. 284-306.

Noyes' communism, Thoreau's treatment of his Montreal experiences, Hawthorne's toying with the magnificence of St. Peter's, all drove at the same simple point from different angles. There was something compellingly attractive about the idea of privacy and self-sufficiency, but in its extreme forms the idea was a *cul-de-sac*. When personality was narrowed by perfection or by transcendence down to a point source of virtue, the individual became a cipher. There was an obvious and hopeless incompleteness about the liberated poet or the perfected saint; the surpassing moral elevation of such an ideal individual made him, in Emerson's phrase, unfit for society. As it existed in America, at any rate, society was not, as Thoreau put it, an "arena" into which such a man could descend. The problem of isolation, then, could find imaginative resolution only in what was, in an American context, radical and unfamiliar.

This outcome was not the ending of a purely intellectual process. Both the preoccupation with the individual and the inability to resolve the problems of transcendence were reflections of the existential situation of the intellectual in America. Emerson's individualism and its attendant problems were a model case. The radical position of *Nature* was a gloss on Emerson's resignation from the ministry. The years in which his theoretical individualism was most extreme were the years of Emerson's most complete vocational and institutional rootlessness. As he molded a new career, with its new layers of social identity, Emerson reverted to his earlier view that "banishment" from society was intolerable. The ideal of the transcendent individual filled more than intellectual needs; it also helped rationalize vocational problems and failures. In his journal of 1840 Thoreau wrote:

> The world is a fit theatre to-day in which any part may be acted. . . . By another spring, I may be a mail carrier in Peru, or a South African planter, or a Siberian exile, or a Greenland whaler, or a settler on the Columbia River, or a Canton merchant, or a soldier in Florida, or a mackeral-fisher off Cape Sable, or a Robinson Crusoe in the Pacific, or a silent navigator of any sea.

The joking list of callings made the same point about the availability of American careers that Thoreau's Montreal narrative made about the availability of American institutions. What was obviously missing from the entry was any reasonably probable vocation that Thoreau might pursue in New England in 1840. All of the possibilities were careers that involved lonely abstraction from American life. The list, which posed as an optimistic assessment of the world as a "theatre," amounted to a negative inventory of American possibilities. Almost any important intellectual of the period could have made the same kind of inventory.[17]

The lack of well-defined, satisfying career possibilities during the decades before the Civil War was not merely a problem of jobs—though for some, like Thoreau or Melville, the difficulty sometimes took the form of practical unemployment. The problem was, rather, one of social relevance, of finding vocations that would be not only intellectually satisfying but also accompanied by a sense of significant role. John Winthrop, when he insisted on "our Community," did so in an unspoken confidence that men of talent and learning would be in substantial control of affairs. To be an intellectual during the first century of American history was almost surely to be a minister. But while the identification of intellectual activity and the ministry remained strong, the relevance of the ministry to the conduct of life faded. By the period of the Revolution, young men began to seek more effective outlets for talent. For the Revolutionary and post-Revolutionary generations, public life replaced the ministry as the most visible and attractive calling for men of intellect. The careers of John Adams, Thomas Jefferson, Phillip Freneau, Joel Barlow, and a score of others like them were rooted in public affairs and politics. By the mid-1820s, however, politics presented an extremely uninviting aspect. The steady decline of the ministry and the increasingly obvious failure of politics as a career resulted in a vocational vacuum. Men—and, as a new ingredient, women— tried to fill the empty space with a crazy-quilt of utopian schemes, "free" churches, and reform movements, all of which had as part of their purpose the creation of a new, informal politics accessible to the intellectual as a thinker, not as a mere ornament to a party's diplomatic service. By and large, the attempts failed and most of the intellectuals of the period simply lacked clearly understood roles. Within such a context, the ideal of transcendence made perfect sense and answered real needs. At the same time,

---

[17] Thoreau, *Writings*, VII, p. 129.

the wistful, even tragic overtones of solitude dramatized a profound sense of alienation among intellectuals, an alienation much
too serious to be relieved by Jacksonian politics.

Herman Melville wrote a near-perfect parable of this situation
in *Pierre, Or the Ambiguities.* Pierre Glendenning, like Hilda in
the *Marble Faun,* was a transcendent individual. He repudiated
his important ancestry, his inheritance, and his calling as young
squire of the family estate. These acts of repudiation were violent
and complete, and they were crowned by Pierre's going into
Nature to converse familiarly with Spirit. Melville occupied about
half the novel making Pierre into a reasonable facsimile of Emerson's poet; the rest was devoted to Pierre's plight after his liberation. Transcendence solved Pierre's moral dilemma—whether to
acknowledge an illegitimate half-sister. But this solution to the
moral problem created the more difficult problem of career. The
question was both familiar and simple: what was Pierre to do
after he stripped himself of social and historical identity? Melville took Pierre out of his familiar woods and meadows into the
city of New York to test the fate of the liberated individual in
society.

The setting for the remainder of the novel was the subject of
Melville's parable, which was a superb capsule history of the
intellectual in America from colonization to the middle of the
nineteenth century. Pierre, intent on a career as a writer, took
rooms for himself, his putative half-sister, and a servant girl in a
building known as the "Church of the Apostles." When it was
built, the old church had been a focal point of New York life,
but the character of the neighborhood had changed and the building was taken over by lawyers. Later, when the neighborhood
changed character again, the lawyers moved out, and the church
was given over to commercial uses. When Pierre brought his
burden of individualized insight to the church, the street floor
was held by merchants; on the upper stories, like Hilda in her
tower in Rome, lived writers and artists who worked in poverty
and wrote for no audience but themselves. In its two earlier
phases the church (and by implication New York and even the
United States) had had at least a semblance of unity, first religious, then legal-political. But the unity had been broken; the
ministers and then the lawyers had moved out and had been

replaced by a split force of merchants below and transcendental-ists, as Melville called them, on the upper floors. The salient characteristics of the transcendental intellectuals were their shabby irrelevance to the waking life of the city and their intel-lectual impotence. Pierre's career in such a setting could be only a groping failure ended by death in prison.[18]

Melville, like Hawthorne, molded the transcendent individual into a tragic shape. Pierre, when he attempted to live a "chrono-metric" (Melville's term for the private and transcendental) life, as opposed to a "horological" (that is, socially defined) life, could come only to the kind of grief experienced by Captain Ahab or Billy Budd. Similarly, the simple moral point of Hawthorne's novels and stories was the futility of any attempt to step into moral privacy, to get outside man's corporate joint-stock of guilt and shortcoming. But the unhappy outcome of attempts at tran-scendence in Hawthorne's and Melville's work does not mean that they were out of sympathy with the ideal. All their prin-cipal heroes and heroines—Ahab, Hester Prynne in *The Scarlet Letter*, Donatello in *The Marble Faun*, and others—could be objects of genuine concern only because of their unsuccessful attempts to become "chronometric." The demand for ethical free-dom for the individual was contradictory, simultaneously noble and absurb, the highest goal and the most futile plight a man could discover.

A principal ingredient of the antinomy, as Melville's parable made clear, was the upper-room disconnection of the intellectual from the apparent triumph of capitalism. American society, as it developed in the nineteenth century, was probably the most fluid and unstructured society in the history of Western civilization. But stable structure had always been essential to the traditional roles of intellect in churches, courts, and universities. Society in the United States was relatively "free," and freedom was a potent value among intellectuals. But freedom both implied and justified a scramble for repute, place, and power, and it became quite evident by the 1830s that men of learning did not have the char-acteristics the scramble seemed to require. By and large, Ameri-can thinkers accepted the notion that men of talent and ideas

---

[18] "The Church of the Apostles" is Book XIX of *Pierre, Or, the Ambiguities* (New York, 1852).

were, and even ought to be, ineffectual in such an unstructured (or, as Emerson called it, *"divided"*) society. "He could not save his brother's soul," wrote Emerson, "Nor pay his brother's debt." The ideal of the transcendent individual was, in part, a compensatory value, a hope that by rejecting society as he found it a man might enter an unchanging, innocent, and altogether uncompetitive realm of sublimity, a counter-reality to the unsteady flux of experience in America.

This intellectual opposition between individual and society was a direct consequence of the widespread acceptance of the idea of transcendence during the period. And this acceptance, in turn, was a less direct reflex of the idealized political economy of capitalism; the mythic figure of the transcendent individual was a moral and esthetic counterpart of the ideal free entrepreneur. In the prevailing academic moral philosophy, taught with very little variation in every American college, ethics were founded on a belief in intuitive conscience, a faculty of mind that functioned in immediate perception of the good, an inner power not dependent on experience and social instruction. The same men who developed this morality of private conscience also wrote the textbooks of political economy, all of which conformed substantially to the ideal of free competition among individualized sellers and buyers in a free-market situation. The man with a private, intuitive "moral sense" was only the free man of enterprise viewed from a different angle. Emerson's poet, who was a radical version of the conscientious man of orthodox moral science, was also a close relative of the theoretical merchant of political economy: "A thought does not dart into the mind of the recluse scholar who rejoices at the discovery of a new truth but I am presently in acquaintance with it and also made wiser. The merchant does not earn a pittance by his commerce without enlarging the wealth of his customers the community." [19]

The greatest intellectual success of capitalist political economy was its theoretical resolution of the apparent conflict between the individual strivings of the entrepreneur and the common weal. This success was won by giving the individual an indirect but functional role in communal progress. In the moral philosophy of the schools, as it was summarized in such durable and popular

[19] Emerson, *Journals,* III, p. 29.

texts as Francis Wayland's *Elements of Moral Science,* there was no real conflict between private conscience and public morality because one of the chief intuitions of conscience was the necessity of the "obligations" arising from social relations. But when the morality of an intuitive "sense" of the good was pressed to its limits, as it was in several versions of transcendentalism, existing social relations became neither obvious nor necessary. The mutation of intuitive but safe "conscience" into a transcendental "I" transformed intuition into a subversive faculty. By and large, the triumph of "free" society, that is of capitalism in an environment lacking historical restraints, had a confusing and displacing effect on American writers and artists during the first half of the century. Whatever avenues to relevant place and role might open up later were not obvious in 1830 or 1850. But there is no logic in history which makes it difficult for the initial victims of a development to accept some of its basic terms. Thus liberation could be just as much a value for the intellectual as (in theory at least) for the merchant. And if the idea of transcendence proved to be dead end, finishing in abstractions like a "religion of love," in wistful but immobile contemplation of Catholicism, or in tragedy, it still remained a primary ethical and artistic value.

Only if the individualistic premises of free society were rejected (as they certainly were not at Oneida or Brook Farm) could the problem be avoided and functional concepts of community be elaborated which would not simply contradict the actual state of society. In the American South, therefore, there could be a real premium on ideas of community constructed out of available social matter and not out of abstractions or foreign symbols. For most of the period between the Revolution and the Civil War, to be sure, Southerners were about as committed to an ideology of individual "freedom" as their countrymen in the North. But as the conflict between free and slave society gained force, some Southerners began to work out an anti-individualism in ethics and political economy as a vehicle for their attack on free society.

One erratic attempt at such a social philosophy was a tract by a young Mississippian, Henry Hughes, published in 1854 under the ambitious title of *Treatise on Sociology, Theoretical and*

Practical. Hughes drew one grand distinction between what he called "free sovereign" and "ordered sovereign" societies or, in simpler terms, between competitive commerce and slavery. The difference, in his jargon, was that in a free society, the interests of men were mutually antagonistic, whereas in a slave society, the interests of men were "syntagonistic." In free society, all relationships among men were trivial and accidental. But the communal, "syntagonistic" relationships of slave society were permanent and real. Hughes, if he had not been so young and from so deep in the South, might have had Emerson's "American Scholar" address of 1837 in mind. Emerson had complained about the fragmented quality of life in America: "The state of society is one in which the members have suffered amputation from the trunk, and strut about so many walking monsters,—a good finger, a neck, a stomach, an elbow, but never a man." But Emerson could propose only esthetic solutions for social problems. Hughes, on the other hand, could accept what he believed were the communal values of life already present in the South. As a consequence he could claim, as Emerson never could, that there was no opposition between society and the scholar, no division comparable to the split in Melville's Church of the Apostles. The disunity between white men and black created unity within the white community, so that power and intellect were effectively joined in the same men and the problem of vocation melted away. In the South, according to Hughes, "the maximum of civil power, wisdom and goodness is realized. All of one race are thinkers. This, by their vocation. They are mentalists." [20]

A much more sophisticated attack on individualism than Hughes's, published in the same year, was George Fitzhugh's *Sociology for the South.* It was no accident that the first American books to carry the word "sociology" in their titles were defenses of slavery. For both Fitzhugh and Hughes there could be no proper sociology of free society because "free society" was, at bottom, a contradiction in terms. Sociology, for both men, implied the study of functioning community, and outside the South there was no community. The philosophical origins of free society lay

---

[20] Hughes, *Treatise on Sociology, Theoretical and Practical* (Philadelphia, 1854), p. 288; Emerson, "The American Scholar," *Works,* I, p. 83.

in John Locke, and, after him, Adam Smith. Both, and all their followers in America and Europe, began with what Fitzhugh thought was the simple error of supposing that analysis could begin with the individual man considered apart from society. Fitzhugh's assertion that society was the only state of nature was as sweeping as it was simple:

> Men, and all other social and gregarious animals, have a community of thought, of motions, instincts and intuitions. The social body is of itself a thinking, acting, sentient being. . . . The great error of modern philosophy is the ignorance or forgetfulness of this fact.

Western Europe and the northern United States, acting out the grand philosophical mistake, had degenerated into a state of social warfare, in which each man was at his fellow's throat every hour of the day. In desperation men in free society had begun to turn to eccentric solutions like socialism, Oneida perfectionism, or Mormonism. Fitzhugh claimed to sympathize with the anxieties that motivated such movements, because each of them grew out of a recognition of the failure of free society. But the system of slavery, as it was practiced in his Virginia, already avoided the costs of freedom without the excesses and the foolishness of the various socialisms.[21]

Like Hughes, Fitzhugh claimed that the South's solution to the problem of community automatically solved the problem of culture. In the North, where morality could be summed up under the single rubric of greed, the highest cultural type was Benjamin Franklin, "low, selfish, atheistic and material." In the South, as in any slave society, culture was continuous with society, not an alien secretion: "Every scholar . . . sees that Greece and Rome were indebted to [slavery] . . . alone for the taste, the leisure and the means to cultivate their heads and their hearts." It made no real difference to Fitzhugh's argument that by almost anyone else's measure culture in the North was superior. His cultural ideal had much more to do with social harmony, and the integration of intellect with the realities of economy and polity, than it did with aesthetic or philosophical excellence. In the South,

---

[21] Fitzhugh, *Sociology for the South, Or the Failure of Free Society* (Richmond, 1854), pp. 34-72; *Cannibals All! Or, Slaves Without Masters* (Richmond, 1857), pp. 132-133.

according to Fitzhugh and to Hughes, letters and leadership were simply different functions of the same homogeneous and united class.[22]

In many ways Fitzhugh's sociology was as antiquated as Filmer, and its antiquity was further burdened by the fact that it was tied to the doomed institution of slavery. But it was also as new as the writers and social theorists from whom Fitzhugh took much of his point of view toward free society—Louis Blanc, Thomas Carlyle (especially the later Carlyle), Charles Kingsley, author of *Alton Locke,* Charles Dickens, and others just as modern and durable. The institutions he was defending did not last a decade beyond the publication of his *Sociology.* But the intellectual brief Fitzhugh prepared became the central theme of a profound intellectual reversal in post-Civil-War America. After 1860, there was an almost wholesale rejection of the ideal of the transcendent individual. This ideal, which had been a pervasive concept among the contemporaries of Emerson, was replaced among American thinkers by variations of Fitzhugh's preoccupation with the concept of community. In 1860 almost every American intellectual outside the South would have agreed that societies of men were aggregates of individuals, that the individuals were prior, in every sense but chronological, to their societies. By 1920 the order of priority, and everything it implied, was reversed. The individual, most intellectuals would have said, was the creature of his society, shaped by it in the most fundamental way, and irrevocably dependent on it in body and in soul. It may be that a majority of Americans held fast to the notion of the self-sufficient individual, especially as it was celebrated in the literature of business success. But among intellectuals, the pronounced drift was away from Emerson's poet or the man of private conscience and toward concepts of man as a thoroughly social product.

In barest outline this development was only a shift in emphasis in answers to the single question of the relationship of individual and society. But intellectual history does not happen in barest outline or to single ideas. Genuine and radical alterations in key ideas do not occur except as integral parts of larger cultural transforma-

22 *Sociology for the South,* pp. 241-242.

tions. The United States experienced such a transformation in culture during the years between, roughly, 1860 and 1920. The failure of individualism was at the heart of the transformation, and a thorough account of the travail of the concept of the transcendent individual would come close to being a complete intellectual history of the period.

This book probes that history. To be more exact, it is a set of probes; it examines in detail the intellectual careers of five leading American thinkers, Charles Sanders Peirce, James Mark Baldwin, Edward Alsworth Ross, Granville Stanley Hall, and Josiah Royce. The limits and failures of individualism were principal themes in the work of each of these men, different as they were in other respects. The major intellectual currents of the period played over them all, and in each case they felt that the conflicts they faced could best be resolved by a rejection of individualism and the generation of concepts of community. They typify in large measure the problems, anxieties, and resolutions encountered or proposed by their contemporaries. It would be easy enough to omit Peirce in favor of Lester Frank Ward. Charles Horton Cooley fit the pattern of thought as neatly as did E. A. Ross. George Herbert Mead's intellectual career followed many of the same lines as James Mark Baldwin's. A list of the intellectuals who would be legitimate subjects for chapters in this book would virtually exhaust the possibilities of the period.

Superficially, the five men whom I have chosen have little in common, aside from the pointless facts that they were all Americans and were active at about the same time. They did not belong to any philosophical school or movement. They were pragmatists, idealists, and positivists. They knew each other's work and in some cases exerted an influence over one another, but their personal contacts were few. The disappearance of any one of them would not have noticeably altered the lives of any of the others. The chapters that follow are therefore marked by a strong concentration on biography, for only a detailed understanding of the diverse ways in which ideas incubated within the minds of particular men can produce an adequate appreciation of the intellectual history of any period. Ideas do not happen; they are had, and they are had by men whose lives and personalities sometimes seem to have idiosyncrasy as their only quality in common.

But history contains unities that its participants were not aware of, and the sternest challenge to the historian is to detect unity where preliminary appearance is one of confusion. For anyone who sets out to write intellectual history, it should be a foregone conclusion that thematic unity is to be found in ideas as much as in such external considerations as institutional connections or geographical proximities. From such a point of view, the fact that an apparently diverse agglomeration of intellectuals shares a common response to a common problem is much more important than concrete association in time and place.

This does not mean, however, that time, place, and circumstance are irrelevant, for intellectual history is a much more complex task than mechanically tracing out the life histories of ideas. This complexity results immediately from the complexity of the divided life that an intellectual (as opposed to an idea) leads. The intellectual, the man who habitually takes thought as his vocation, spends his energies and consciousness in two worlds. He lives in a world of ideas where the most important events are scientific theories, new modes in art, or new social and political theories. In this realm of ideas, time and space are elastic; the otherwise stubborn facts of history and geography bend under the pressure of intellect and imagination. Duns Scotus can be as "present" to the twentieth-century intellectual as Whitehead; Plato and Bergson have a kind of contemporaneity. The pace of events is leisurely and controlled; the environment is normally friendly; and the dangers are usually few, even to peace of mind. But the intellectual also lives in a world of affairs. War and peace, the vicissitudes of politics, elections, labor problems, and racial strife bear in upon him. Perhaps even more important, he shares with the carpenter or the bond salesman the problems of making a career and getting and spending a living, having (or not having) a family, accommodating himself to governments and neighbors. This divided life endows the intellectual with what Emerson once called a "double consciousness," an awareness of two radically different kinds of experience which must be somehow kept in adjusted relation.

Occasionally an intellectual will claim to accept and even to celebrate as complete as possible a dissociation between mind and the world. To all but beggars and mystics (and among them only to ideal types) a genuine bifurcation of experience into unrelated streams of intellect and event is intolerable. For most intellectuals involves an attempt to hold the two faces of experience in some kind of manageable tension. The very quick of the life of an intellectual is that sensitive area where ideas and affairs join or conflict. When intellect and event collide, either ideas or facts have to be altered so that experience as a whole has at least a semblance of integration.

The integration of the life of the mind and the world of affairs is difficult to maintain. From time to time, the intellectual's world view—his complex set of beliefs about God, man, and the nature of the universe—view is disturbed when he encounters an unfamiliar idea. Or his accommodation to the world of facts is upset by a political revolution or an alteration in some institution in which he is involved. He must either alter his world-view to take account of a new set of facts or he must seek to alter the factual conditions of his life to fit a newly acquired feature of his intellectual landscape. What historians call "periods" in intellectual history are defined by generalized challenges to intellectuals' precarious efforts to keep the two sides of their consciousness internally stable and in relative harmony with each other. In the United States, between the middle of the nineteenth century and the 1920s, there was a powerful double challenge, a threat to both poles of the intellectual's existence, which gave the period its singular air of constant change and uncertainty.

On the one hand, intellectuals were deprived of a stable world view by the implications of evolution. In several forms, Darwinian, Spencerian and Hegelian, evolutionary theories convinced one thinker after another that man was, in origin, at least, an animal, that the world was altogether in process, and that categories and ideals that had been presumed to stable were subject to change. Evolutionary ideas penetrated into every corner of the world of learning, every department of the universities. Psychology, sociology, anthropology, ethics, philosophy, even logic, paid a heavy intellectual tribute to biology. In the beginning there was a tendency among Americans to blink the challenge of evolutionary ideas, to interpret Darwin, according to Spencer or Hegel, as a new justification for old optimisms. But after the initial absorption of evolutionary theory, it became obvious that a Darwinian view of the world, unless it could be hedged and modified, threatened familiar concepts of man and society.

The second threat is more difficult to define concretely, though more obvious in a matter-of-fact way. The economic and technological revolution that the United States endured had subtle and varied effects on American intellectuals. On the most obvious level, it forced them to think in new terms about their society. But industrialism had more intimate consequences; it created an essentially new kind of university, a set of institutions that absorbed almost all the leading minds of the period. In comparison with the preceding generation American intellectuals who matured after 1860 were radically institutionalized. They had a well-defined nexus with their society, something an Emerson or a Melville had lacked. In society at large industrialism began to reverse the process of institutional atrophy so typical of the first half of the century. This demanded of intellectuals new perceptions of society and of the relationship between society and the man of learning.

Together, evolutionary concepts and the rough facts of industrialization and urbanization established the unifying intellectual issues of the day, and these two challenges did not operate separately. Evolution and economic change converged on the intellectual and professional careers of American thinkers, and their convergence threw into relief the most pervasive problem of the period—the hopeless insufficiency of the isolated individual. Both evolutionary ideas and economic and social realities made it apparent, in many different and varied ways, that man could not stand alone, in what James Mark Baldwin called his "isolated majesty," apart from other men. It became painfully clear that men were the products and not the wilfully compacting constituents of their species and their society. There was an urgent demand for concepts of man that gave him protective membership in a social community that stood as a buffer between the individual and the harsh uncertainties of both the evolutionary and the industrial world.

It was this need that the intellectuals who are the subjects of this book tried to meet. The common theme of their quest for community joins their otherwise disparate careers. Their lives were different, and they encountered evolution and industrial

America in different guises and circumstances. Thus their critiques of individualism varied broadly in detail and tone. But to each of them the idea of community seemed the best response to the disintegrating effects of evolution and industrial capitalism that threatened both their minds and their society.

Chapter 2

Charles Sanders Peirce: The Community of Inquiry

On the evening of November 12, 1863 the High School Association of Cambridge, Massachusetts gathered in annual reunion to hear an oration by a youthful Cambridge neighbor, Charles Peirce, on "The Place of Our Age in the History of Civilization." Aside from his parentage (he was the son of the famous Harvard mathematician, Benjamin Peirce), the speaker was not especially noteworthy. He was barely twenty-four years old and just out of Harvard. His subject was, if anything, even more commonplace. For a generation "the present age" had been a favorite theme for New England orators from Emerson to schoolboys. And the Civil War had made comforting assessments of "our age" even more popular than before. The members of the Association could only have expected to hear a conventional address full of praise for the nineteenth century, for its masterful accomplishments in science and technology, and for its progress in the uplifting of humanity. If he followed a conventional pattern, the young speaker would probably pause to notice the war, but somehow he would be able to treat it as only an unfortunately violent chapter in the progress of civilization. He would probably complain a little about the "materialism" of the age as well, but this complaint, too, would be finally submerged in affirmation.[1]

Peirce began in orthodox fashion. He gave his audience a conventional estimate of the virtues of the age—a healthy-minded

---

[1] The address was printed in the *Cambridge Chronicle*, November 21, 1863.

skepticism in philosophy and science and a strong but controlled spirit of liberty in human affairs. He also recounted the historical career of the Western world in terms familiar to everyone. All the great ages of the past, the Rise of Christianity, the Establishment of the Modern Nations, the Reformation, and so on, had been but a prelude to the Age of Reason, "Our Age," now verging toward fruition. This comfortable, almost ritual, exercise in history brought Peirce nearly to the end of his address. But then he began to talk in an odd way about the *end* of the Present Age. He even called out for its end. "Our age," he said, "is brilliant, and apparently confident of its own eternity." But it had to end because it was terribly flawed, because its chief concern was with mere material convenience and welfare. The characteristic advances of the century, steam and electricity, and all the devices they entailed had their place, but "toying" with them ought not to be man's main preoccupation. Then Peirce voiced the famous Emersonian plaint:

> Web to weave, and corn to grind,
> Things are in the saddle,
> And ride mankind[2]

The lines were already part of the vocabulary of literate New Englanders, and they probably were taken as an oratorical feint, a dramatic hesitation to heighten the effect of a peroration placing the balance of accounts firmly to the credit of nineteenth-century civilization. But Peirce violated custom by *insisting* on the Emersonian gesture, making it the center of an unambiguous call for a new kind of culture whose fundamental sentiments and faiths would be not merely different from but opposed to the faiths and sentiments of the Age.

Peirce in 1863 was much younger and less experienced than the Emerson who wrote *Nature* in the middle of the 1830s. And Peirce did not have Emerson's rhetorical poise and sense of audience. But he was trying in a somewhat clumsy way to force an intellectual moment very similar to the one that Emerson had created in *Nature*. Like Emerson, he was assessing his civilization, finding it not merely frayed but fundamentally misguided, and trying to envision a kind of experience radically different from

---

[2] The lines were from Emerson's "Ode to W. H. Channing."

the experience available in society as he found it. Both men were concerned about the ways in which the values and habits of the Age cut men off from what Peirce called "converse," and Emerson "original relation," with the cosmos. Both men assumed the existence of a real and harmonious order in nature, an esthetic order accessible to liberated insight. "Ah!" Peirce ended his address, "what a heavenly harmony will be that when all the sciences, one as a viol, another as a flute, another as a trumpet, shall peal forth in that majestic symphony of which the noble organ of astronomy forever sounds the theme." And, for both Emerson and Peirce, the "heavenly harmony" was not merely a genteel ideal to be piously and timidly alluded to on ceremonial occasions. It was a real and pressing alternative to life as they found it, to what Emerson called the "din and craft of the street," and Peirce the "tinkering" and "toying" mentality of the century.

For Peirce, as for Emerson, the underlying perfection and harmony of nature was built on what Peirce called the "inward existence" of every natural fact. And inward existence required a special form of perception. Using what they thought of as science, men in the present age could only "observe" nature. But when the Present Age had done its work and when men broke free of its illusions, Peirce thought they would gain "communion" with Nature, no longer seeing it as an affair of "uses" (what Emerson had called "commodity") but as an "esthetic" reality, "infinite and amiable." In the Present Age, said Peirce, it was the poet who personified everything in nature, who professed love for the stone and the drop of water. In his response to nature the poet was a prophet of what the true science would be. A new and genuine science would enlarge, and so replace, the poet's insight: "But the time is coming when there shall be no more poetry, for that which was poetically divined shall be scientifically known." The work of the new science would be to pierce through to the esthetic heart of nature, beyond observation and use, beyond even insight into the "inward existence" of particular natural facts, to a luxurious perception of the "heavenly harmony" of the cosmos as a whole.

The possibility of such a perception required an ethical decision. Emerson's poet had to "retire" from chamber and society, to relinquish the ordinary ownership of things in order to gain that ecstatic dissolution of the self which was the triumphant outcome of his venture into nature. Peirce's "esthetic" man had to perform a similar act of self-denial. Before men could have communion with perfection, they had to love it. They had to be converted away from a preoccupation with the self (of which the Present Age's conception of science as useful was only an extension) and must instead profess the "kingdom of Christ" in all of nature. Even in the Present Age, Christianity secreted the truth that "man was not made to turn his eye inward." But Christianity had degenerated into a set of dogmas and into mere injunctions to visit widows and to keep oneself "unspotted from the world." Peirce predicted that a new Christianity, elevated into a selfless love for all being, would soon "transfuse" itself through all of human society. This wholesale conversion of the "nation" and the "races" would usher in that new age to which science had only the methodological keys. Lured by poetic divinations and elevated by love, science could come finally to the truth, which would, in turn, be both good and beautiful.

During the half-century that followed this youthful and sanguine Cambridge address, Peirce developed into the most able and inventive American philosopher of the nineteenth century. He never published a philosophical book, and he never held a major academic post—or even a minor one for more than a few years. But by the 1890s he had generated a subterranean and somewhat mysterious reputation that would force almost any young intellectual to think of him as a "big man."[3] He exerted a

---

[3] The phrase "big man" was used by the sociologist E. A. Ross to describe Peirce. A sense of the kind of mysterious but large reputation Peirce had was contained in an account left by a student of William James. The year was 1907: "One day, the landlady asked [the student] to come into one of the rooms to see an old gentleman, who had been ill and was very likely dying. When he went in, he saw a sick, worn body of a man obviously suffering from undernourishment and lack of care; and when asked his name, he was told 'Charles Peirce.' In a wild confusion of emotions [he] and a friend went to find William James, and caught him coming out of class. James listened to their story. 'Why,' he said, his face changing, 'I owe him everything!' and swung into a cab to call for Peirce and take him home." Murial Rukeyser, *Willard Gibbs* (Garden City, New York, 1942), p. 378. Quoted in Joseph Lancaster Brent, "A Study of the Life of Charles Sanders Peirce, "Unpublished dissertation, University of California at Los Angeles, 1960. Brent's dissertation is by far the best single source of biographical material on Peirce.

powerful sway, if not an influence in a precise sense, over philosophers as different in their intellectual commitments as Josiah
Royce and William James, and during the twentieth century,
Peirce has become widely acknowledged as the most original
American philosopher of his period. The breadth of his appeal to
his contemporaries and to later intellectuals has been due, in part
at least, to the fact that his essays and published fragments do
not seem to fall neatly into a philosophical system, so that he has
been many things to many men. The twentieth-century logician
can find ample evidence to show that Peirce was a forerunner of
modern logical posivitism or empiricism. Pragmatists and instru-
mentalists have always claimed Peirce as a founder of their movement. But an absolute idealist like Royce was able to find crucial
sustenance for his own intellectual views in Peirce's writings.

Peirce's philosophy was held together, however, by a consistent
motive, if not by clearly stated principles, and the 1863 oration
announced what this motive would always be. Peirce thought of
truth as an ideal value, quite distinct from any practical uses to
which men might put the results of inquiry. Men might be driven
to inquire by all sorts of personal needs—pain, greed, a longing
for control of their world—but these motives did not invest the
truth with its value. "No human prudence," he once wrote, "can
long arrest the triumphal car of truth—no, not if the discovery
were such as to drive every member of the race to suicide."[4] The
worth of the truth was not present and prudential, but final and
ideal. Peirce believed, against a great deal of intellectual pressure
from Darwinism and other intellectual currents of the day, in final
causes or purposes in nature. The ideal, final cause of the world
as a whole was perfect "harmony." Truth, the final cause of all
inquiry, was "communion" with perfection.

The antithesis to truth as "communion" was men's ordinary
preoccupation with themselves and their private interests. Peirce
insisted, therefore, that genuine science could come only as a result of moral decision, that men had to be converted to science in
the same way that in religious experience they were converted

---

[4] "The Order of Nature," *Popular Science Monthly* (1878), in *Collected
Papers of Charles Sanders Peirce*, Arthur W. Burks, Charles Hartshorne, and Paul Weiss, eds. (Second edition, eight vols., Cambridge,
1960), 6.426. It is customary to cite the *Collected Papers* by volume and
paragraph. Thus "6.426" refers to volume six, paragraph 426.

to the love of God. He liked to say that logic, or the method of science, was based on ethics. And the ethical decision involved in a conversion to science was nothing short of a complete facing about from the normal human concern with the self to a love for the world at large. Here lay the secret of salvation from the tragic limits of men's finite and petty lives. This evangelical desire to save men from themselves lay behind all of Peirce's many papers on logic and epistemology. For him there was no technical question of philosophy which did not force, in the end, a moral choice. The typical strategy of his philosophical essays was to employ a formal critique of the logic of knowledge and inquiry to show, at last, that the validity of the method of science depended on the ethical stance of the inquirer, on his complete commitment to truth as a value that transcended every short-run purpose and practical use.

For this philosophical motive Peirce was drawing on an ethic of science deeply imbedded in his own family, indeed in all of literary New England at mid-century. His father was a mathematician who thought of his discipline as a pathway to a realm of ideals where even the square root of minus one really existed. In his classroom Benjamin Peirce was fond of stepping back from a blackboard demonstration to say, "Gentlemen, there must be a God!" At the end of one of his formal papers on mathematics, he defined the "object of geometry" as

> to penetrate the veil of material forms, and disclose the thoughts which lie beneath them . . . and when our researches are successful, when a generous and heaven-eyed inspiration has elevated us above humanity, and raised us triumphantly into the very presence of the divine intellect, how instantly and entirely are human pride and vanity repressed, and, by a single glance at the glories of the infinite mind are we humbled to the dust.[5]

Benjamin Peirce's friend and colleague, the zoologist Louis Agassiz, who was probably the best-known scientist in America before the Civil War, once characterized biology, in much the same way, as "intercourse with the Highest Mind." In their conception of science as "communion" with perfection Agassiz and the Peirces,

---

[5] Brent, "A Study of the Life of Charles Sanders Peirce," p. 31. The best study of Benjamin Peirce is Sven Peterson, "Benjamin Peirce, Mathmatician and Philosopher," *Journal of the History of Ideas,* 16 (January, 1955), pp. 89-112.

both father and son, were dealing in counter-realities of an Emersonian sort, portraying the life of the mind as one "elevated" to a consoling harmony, above the world of ordinary experience, clear of vanity and self-interest. They were exemplars of what George Santayana called the genteel tradition in American letters. They regarded ideas as ideals that might compensate men for the failings of the self and the world, as what Santayana called "Sabbath" experiences, alternative to the "weekday" concerns of businessmen, soldiers, mechanics and farmers.[6]

With this conception of science and of what should count as important knowledge in general went a corresponding conception of the style that ought to be cultivated by an intellectual. In a radical form the pursuit of purely Sabbath experience lent a sense of career to Emerson's poet, or to the life of a Garrison, or to the bitter experience of Melville's Pierre. But the notion that intellectual activity ought to be elevated away from the ordinary course of experience was also widely domesticated to fit the more commonplace experience of the typical minister or college professor. Such men shared with the poet an insight into morality. Indeed such insight was their stock in trade in nineteenth-century America, but they contained insight within institutions, working out quiet careers in their churches and colleges. As a group, the ministers and the college teachers (men moved easily between the two vocations) constituted the nearest thing in the United States to an institutionalized intellecual class. A few of them, such as Mark Hopkins at Williams College and James McCosh at Princeton, became famous outside the boundaries of their towns and colleges. For the most part they fed on local status, but collectively they controlled the schools and churches not only of New England but also of the rest of the country. Gradually, during the century, the kinds of institutional power they had grew faded and threadbare. They came to think of themselves and of men of letters generally as beleaguered guardians, almost feminine in their stance, of ideals in a world gone mad for "materialism." In their defense the vague idealism of "elevation," high purpose, and special moral insight was the stuff of identity and the fabric of rhetoric.

---

[6] Santayana, *Character and Opinion in the United States* (New York, 1920), pp. 4-7.

During the latter half of the century, notions of what knowledge ought to be, and, correspondingly, of what an intellectual ought to be, underwent a drastic change. The emphasis shifted (to oversimplify the matter considerably) from moral insight to matter-of-fact knowledge, from Emerson's poet, at one extreme, to Thorstein Veblen's "engineer" at the other. Peirce's generation wrought the change and, as a result, found itself caught in a very serious division of loyalties and aspirations. On the one hand, the genteel conception of intellect as a Sabbath affair continued to be compelling. On the other hand, the frayed life of semi-poverty and dwindling effectiveness led by the old-style teachers and ministers became increasingly uninviting. New disciplines in the natural sciences and more importantly in social science held out the possibility that intellectuals could deal with subjects more obviously relevant to society than the inherited body of theology and moral philosophy. And these disciplines seemed to require that the intellectual relinquish or at least mask the moral stance.

The pull of these contrary notions of what an intellectual career ought to be—a defense of ideality or scientific aggression upon culture—brought serious ambiguities into the lives and work of almost all of Peirce's contemporaries. The choice between them, which was seldom made clearly, occupied the minds of men like William Graham Sumner, Henry Adams, Richard T. Ely, William James, Josiah Royce—of almost every intellectual who matured after about 1860 and who did a substantial part of his work before the turn of the century. Looking backward over the generation with which he had matured, John Dewey once summed up their collective experience very neatly: "Modern science, modern industry and politics, have presented us with an immense amount of material foreign to, and often inconsistent with, the most prized intellectual heritage of the western world. This is the cause of our modern intellectual perplexities."[7] More exactly still, as Dewey himself said more than once, the primary inconsistency was between science and mortality, both as bodies of knowledge and as callings pursued by intellectuals.

Most of Peirce's contemporaries hedged the question. They attempted to be men of science and still to maintain the air of earnestness on ethical questions that had been the badge of func-

[7] John Dewey, *Experience and Nature* (New York, 1958), ix.

tion for their college and pulpit predecessors. Part of the hedge required them to cultivate new kinds of careers. Primarily, they helped make the colleges over from citadels of orthodoxy at bay into something resembling the modern university. By this means they created the first important new matrix for intellectual careers since the politics of the Revolution. A career as a university scientist or social scientist (the vocation which absorbed a majority of the significant intellectuals of the post-Civil War generation) required a new kind of training and a new kind of skill. A German Ph.D., or at least some years of study in Europe, was one near prerequisite. And with it went the other—competence in some sort of empirical technique, whether in the chemistry laboratory, in what William James called brass-instrument psychology, in new statistical techniques, or new historical methods. But still there lingered over this first generation of university professors the air of the old courses in mental and moral philosophy that had been at the heart of the ante-bellum college. No matter what their ethical positions were—Sumner's rather hard-bitten *laissez-faire* morality, Lester Frank Ward's state positivism, or the simple humaneness of William James—their science issued in ethical precept. It was, in fact, a simple matter to find new justification for most of what Dewey called the "prized heritage," to merely set the older morality of the college teacher or the minister on a new base. On the whole, the new empirical psychology was a critique of the old notion of the soul, biology was a critique of Revelation, and anthropology a critique of Providence. But, characteristically, the same men who pressed the new disciplines forward were still able to find new rationales for old ideals of right, duty, and charity.

Peirce in 1863 was announcing that his philosophical strategy would have nothing about it of such hedge or straddle. He would not (and he managed to insist publicly on this position until the end of his life) set the old ethics of ideality on a scientific base. Instead, he would insist without a hint of compromise that science *itself* was a moral undertaking and that the truth remained, in Santayana's language, an utterly "Sabbath" ideal. Peirce knew more of science than most of his generation and more of scientific method than any of them (save perhaps one or two men in Europe) but he refused to regard natural or social science as a source of ethical values. He attempted, instead, to reinterpret the methods of science so they would *depend* on such ideals as "communion," "heavenly harmony," and the "lever of love."

This insistence entailed both a certain concept of the way an intellectual, or, in Peirce's language, an "inquirer," ought to regard his calling and a mechanism through which the calling might be worked out. Both the conception of calling and the mechanism of performance were so elevated that they were unworkable (except as ironic standards with which to identify failure), but they were the touchstones of Peirce's philosophy from the 1860s to his death in 1914. Toward the end of his career he summed up the ethic of being an inquirer in language that did not differ much from the address of 1863:

> The very first command that is laid upon you becomes, as everybody knows, to recognize a higher business than your business, not merely an avocation after the daily task of your vocation is performed, but a generalized conception of duty which completes your personality by melting it into the neighboring parts of the universal cosmos.[8]

The conception of calling was very much like Emerson's program for the poet, and it carried with it the same problem—how to make such a "command" workable, how to build around it a set of instructions for conduct. Peirce came no nearer a working solution to the problem than Emerson, but he altered the Emersonian schema of salvation in a way that almost summarizes the difference between the two generations' intellectual experience. "Solitude" and "nature" had been Emerson's opening moves. For solitude in nature Peirce substituted the notion of membership in an infinite "community of inquiry." Men, he said, were "mere cells in the social organism," and could gain real existence only by affirming their loyalty to the community of all men who inquire after the truth. The individual was merely a "negation," the embodiment of ignorance and error. The community, on the other hand, was the vehicle of truth and the only hope of communion with the cosmos. The choice between the individual and the community, according to Peirce, was absolute. There could be no harmony between the private self and the community, since any affirmation of the self was a denial of the community. This choice was the supreme issue of both philosophy and life. "Whether the *community* [Peirce usually capitalized or italicized

---

[8] "On Detached and Vitally Important Topics As Such," a lecture of 1898, in *Collected Papers*, 1.673.

the word] is to be considered an end in itself" was "the most
fundamental practical question in regard to every public institution."[9] For the transcendent individual of the Emersonian generation he substituted a transcendent community. The end remained
more or less the same, an original relation with nature, but the
means were completely revised. Whereas Emerson had dropped
"society" out of relation between "self" and "cosmos," Peirce made
"community" an ideal large enough to contain both the individual
and the world.

Peirce's first formal exposition of his concept of community was
a series of articles in the magazine of St. Louis Hegelianism,
The Journal of Speculative Philosophy, in 1868. In three beauti-
fully wrought and radically conceived essays Peirce argued that
individuality was a mere illusion and urged his readers to com-
mit themselves to total, self-denying membership in the community of men. "The individual man," Peirce concluded the second essay, "since his separate existence is manifested only by
ignorance and error, so far as he is anything apart from his fellows, and from what he and they are to be, is only a negation."[10]
In tone and style the essays were in large part *cris de coeur*, gaining force as much from Peirce's passion as from his reasonings.
But, always the logician, Peirce adduced one formal argument
after another for his view.

His most radical tactic was to challenge traditional concepts of
the self and the way it experienced the world. In "questions"
modeled on early Scholastic arguments Peirce attacked the idea
that the human self was something given to rather than gained
from experience, something innate and therefore capable of being
purely private and personal. Even self-consciousness, that for-
midable bastion of individualistic psychologies and epistemol-
ogies, was, Peirce argued, the result of experience and error in
a social world, not of any kind of *a priori* cognitive process. In
every respect, then, a man was the product of his experience of
the external world.[11]

---

[9] Peirce, Review of Alexander Campbell Fraser's edition of *The Works of
George Berkeley*, in *North American Review* (1871), *Collected Papers*, 8.11.
[10] "Some Consequences of Four Incapacities," *Journal of Speculative Philosophy* (1868), in *Collected Papers*, 5.317.
[11] "Questions Concerning Certain Faculties Claimed for Man," *Ibid.*, 5.213-
263.

This radical empiricism was a rejection of Peirce's first philosophical master, Kant, whom he had been disciplined to read several hours a day as a boy. But Peirce did not merely retreat from Kant in order to defend the more popular trenches dug by British empiricism. He gave experience a new twist, a dynamic and continuous quality missing from the simpler empiricisms of the day. Peirce made it his central premise that every cognition, every awareness, conscious sensation or reasoning, was determined by previous cognitions. There were no "simple" ideas determined by their objects alone that could be built by the gentle force of association into a static web of knowledge. Instead, every act of knowing was a moment in a continuous stream of experience, a moment irrevocably conditioned by previous moments.[12]

When a man looks at a white wall, Peirce's most modern and striking argument ran, he seems to see an unbroken expanse of white. If he closes one eye, the effect is still the same. But it is physically impossible for the man to see what he thinks he sees, for there is a blind spot on the retina of his eye, a circle of insensate darkness where neither light nor color are perceived. The fact that the man thinks he sees a solid expanse of white and not a while doughnut shape is proof that his cognition is determined by his previous cognitions. In this case the man's experience is unconsciously shaped in the most fundamental way by his habit, built up since infancy, of mentally compensating for the blind spot on the retina. In the same manner, Peirce argued, all cognitions, all moments of conscious experience, were determined by previous cognitions. Nothing, he concluded, was ever seen or thought afresh. Consciousness was a continuous, seamless stream of cognitive moments.[13]

In the language that he tried to build for himself over the years Peirce called each cognitive moment in experience a "sign." Each sign was determined by previous signs and, in turn, each helped determine some future sign. Man, since he was progressively defined by the content of his consciousness, was himself a sign and shared all the properties of signs. Then Peirce struck

---

[12] "Questions Concerning Certain Faculties Claimed for Man," especially 5.259-263.
[13] *Ibid.*, 5.220.

his boldest blow and the one least justified by his arguments. To
have meaning a sign had to address itself to future signs. This
criterion of meaning applied, he claimed, to man as well as to
any other sign. Unless a man addressed his thoughts to the future
thoughts of other men, he had no meaning, hence, no real existence as a conscious, intelligent being. Unless the future object of
a man's thoughts was the thought of an infinite community of
other thinkers, sooner or later he would lose meaning and existence altogether. He would become, in Peirce's term, a negation.[14]
Thus Peirce made the acknowledgment of the community the
condition of any man's very existence. He made immortality and
conscious life inseparable. Only by gaining a species of immortality, membership in an infinite community, could man breathe
life into his own existence. If the stream of a man's experience
were cut at the physical and temporal boundaries of his own existence, then that existence was, in an ultimate sense, thoughtless,
a mere lacuna in the stream of thought at large.

The chief problem of philosophy and of life for Peirce was to
discover the proper method to unite men into a genuine community. The method he advocated was logic (in a very broad
sense), and the nexus between man and the community was the
truth, an inevitable product of logicality. A man might have true
cognitions, referring to real objects, or false cognitions, referring
to nothing at all. No individual man, no matter how wise or
learned, could ever know whether his conceptions of things were
true, how far he grasped reality, or, as a result, how real he was.
The truth, and, hence, reality itself, was accessible only to a community of inquirers, infinite in number, and capable of carrying
on inquiry for an infinitely long time. In the ideal end such a
community would inevitably find the truth and thus experience
reality. For the individual, painfully and foolishly groping about
in ignorance and error, no truth was possible, but by using the
methods of logic and science, methods fated to hit upon the
truth eventually, the individual man could compensate for his
ignorance and error. A man's redemption did not depend on his
actually being in possession of the truth about any particular
matters of fact, but on his loyalty to a method of reasoning that
would, when faithfully employed by an infinite number of other

14 "Some Consequences of Four Incapacities," 5.283-317.

men, inevitably reveal the truth about all matters of fact. Here was the conjunction of love and logic on which Peirce insisted throughout his intellectual career.[15]

Love and logic converged most concretely on the problem of chance. Most of the practical judgments men make in the world, Peirce believed, were probable inferences—that such and such was probably the case or probably would happen. In actual fact any individual man experienced only a minute part of the universe, and even the totality of men had thus far explored only a small corner of the cosmos. But from their severely limited experience, men extrapolated educated opinions about the nature of the whole universe. All human science was the result of the examination of a tiny sample of matter, time and space, with the added assumption that what held true of the sample would hold true of the whole. Peirce regarded it as almost "magical" that men could thus reason about what they had not experienced, could make a leap of intellect from the accessible past and present to the unknown, the distant, and the future. The logical grounds on which such reasoning might be valid seemed to Peirce to be the "lock upon the door of philosophy."[16]

---

[15] "Consequences of Four Incapacities," 5.311; "Grounds of Validity of the Laws of Logic: Further Consequences of Four Incapacities," *Journal of Speculative Philosophy* (1869), in *Collected Papers*, 5.318-357.

[16] All cognitions, Peirce maintained, were the results of inferences. Inferences he divided into the analytic and the synthetic. Analytic inferences were of the familiar deductive form—all A are B; this is an A; hence, this is a B. Granted the premises, the conclusions of such inferences were certain. According to Peirce, there were two kinds of synthetic inferences, the inductive and the hypothetical. Inductive was the familiar progress from particulars to a general rule—this is an A; this is a B; hence, all A are (probably) B. Hypothesis, which Peirce sometimes called abduction, was reasoning from a particular, through a general rule, to another particular—this is a B; all A are B; hence, this is (probably) an A. Peirce believed that only induction and hypothesis revealed or suggested new knowledge, so it became imperative for him to justify them, since their justification was the justification of the method of science. This problem, he thought, was logically precedent to Kant's "How are synthetic judgements *a priori* possible?" According to Peirce, if it could be shown that synthetic judgments were possible at all, let alone *a priori*, then the answer to Kant's query would come readily. Cf. "Induction, Deduction and Hypothesis," *Popular Science Monthly* (1878), in *Collected Papers*, 2.619-631; "Grounds of Validity of Laws of Logic," 6.341-348. On Peirce and Kant, see James Feibleman, *An Introduction to Peirce's Philosophy*, (New York, 1946) ch. 2, and the early chapters of Murray G. Murphey, *The Development of Peirce's Philosophy* (Cambridge, 1961).

The usual explanation given in Peirce's day for the apparent validity of probable inferences was that nature was "regular" and that knowing a part of the universe was, for all practical purposes, the same as knowing all of it. Peirce rejected the argument from the regularity of nature and with it the whole sanguine positivism of John Stuart Mill and his followers. Instead, Peirce argued, the truth of probable judgments about the world could depend only on the presumed existence of an infinite community of inquirers. At no particular time could any individual man know whether his contingent judgments were true. But collectively, men and other intelligent beings could know that "in the long run our errors balance one another." The community, unlike the individual or any finite number of individuals, might exist forever and could test every guess, disprove every false hypothesis, and reach a firm decision on what was true and real. By making his predictions (which was, for Peirce, the same as living his life) on behalf of the community, a man did not improve his chances of being correct about any particular question of fact, but he did make it certain that his enterprise would succeed in the long run.[17]

The commitment which Peirce urged men to make to the community was essentially religious. Institutionally, he was a half-hearted Episcopalian, with little or no interest in church matters, but he was a congenital and incurable minister. His finest essays were sermons in logic and scientific method, relentless in the rigor of their technical exegesis, but edged with a passion that transformed logic into an evangel's message of love. Peirce believed with a prophet's fervor that only the "revelation" of the "saving power" of the community could "redeem the logicality of all men." The price of this redeeming grace was high—the ultimate self-sacrifice of Gethsemane. But "He who would not sacrifice his soul to gain the whole world, is illogical in all his inferences collectively." And for Peirce, to be illogical was to be damned.[18]

The religious, supra-logical character of Peirce's ideal of community became obvious in a series of essays he published in the *Popular Science Monthly* in 1877-1878, "Illustrations of the Logic

[17] "Grounds of Validity of Laws and Logic," 5.354.
[18] *Ibid.*, 5.354-356.

of Science." The first two essays, "The Fixation of Belief" and "How to Make Our Ideas Clear," were later made famous by William James, who hailed them as the first statement of the philosophy of pragmatism. But Peirce at the time intended these two essays only as preliminary exercises to clear away tangled brush. In Peirce's estimate "The Fixation of Belief" and "How to Make Our Ideas Clear" did not even cross the threshold of scientific logic. "It is important," he concluded the second essay, "to know how to make our ideas clear, but they may be ever so clear without being true. How to make them so, we have next to study."[19] Making ideas true, as opposed to merely clear, was, of course, the task and justification of the community of inquiry. Peirce's analysis of the way probable judgments had to depend on the community was generally the same as it had been in the *Journal of Speculative Philosophy* series in 1868, but the tone in which he exhorted men to acknowledge the community was more insistent, his arguments more extreme and drastic, and the radicalism of his position much closer to the surface.

The denouement of the *Popular Science Monthly* series was what appeared to be a rash hypothetical problem, posed as much to shock as to persuade. Give a man two decks of twenty-six cards each, Peirce mused. Tell him that one deck contains twenty-five red cards and only one black, the other deck contains twenty-five black cards and only one red. Promise the man, as though you were God himself, that if he can draw a red card from either deck he may choose, his immortal soul will be spared. Most any practical man, Peirce assumed, would draw from the predominately red deck, supposing his chances of getting a red card to be very good indeed. But, on occasion, some one will draw the single black card from the red deck. He had erred, and erred so badly that his very immortal soul is lost forever.[20]

The problem, and for Peirce it was a most pressing problem, was to give this poor unfortunate assurance that he had not gambled in vain. Peirce believed that all men were, at all times, gamblers in a universe of chance. The most distinctive fact about

---

[19] "How to Make Our Ideas Clear," *Popular Science Monthly* (1878), in *Collected Papers*, 5.410.
[20] "The Doctrine of Chances," *Popular Science Monthly* (1878), in *Collected Papers*, 2.652-654.

men's lives was the existence of their errors. And, since truth was
the supreme value, to be in error was to be lost, negated. The
only way to live the life of a truly intelligent being, Peirce
claimed, was to live it wholeheartedly as a member of the community. When faced with the choice of decks, the gamble for
his soul, a man ought to draw not in his own interest but in disinterested devotion to the community's quest for truth. His only
concern ought to be to draw, that is, to live his life, in such a
way that his gambles would contribute to the discovery, in the
long run, of the truth about the cards—that is, the world. A man
who achieved such an attitude of devoted self-denial would suffer
no disappointment at drawing the black card. His personal loss
would be but a step toward a different kind of salvation, the salvation of the community.

Peirce compared this demanding gospel of redemption to St.
Paul's "famous trio of Charity, Faith and Hope." The "logical
sentiments" connected with the community were, Peirce claimed,
a call for interest in an unlimited community (charity); recognition of the possibility that such an interest could become any
man's supreme, exclusive concern (faith); and confidence in the
possible unlimited continuation of intellectual activity by the community (hope). The New Testament, although it might not be the
best available textbook on formal logic, was certainly the highest
authority on the "disposition of heart that man ought to cultivate."
This was what logic finally meant for Peirce, a disposition of
heart, an incredibly fervent and constant denial of private goals
and ambitions, and an equally incredible piety toward the community and its object, the truth.[21]

It is a classic irony that it should have been Peirce who formulated the most thoroughgoing and radical ideal of community in
American or European letters. His life, though it began in a family
that was very much a part of the dense social, intellectual, and institutional life around Harvard, was one of progressive isolation
and alienation from the experience of his generation and from
society at large. Peirce ended in a poverty and isolation which was
a bitter joke on his ideal of community. At the outset, he seemed
to have all the credentials that would assure him a place in Cam-

---

[21] "The Doctrine of Chances," 2.655.

bridge, Harvard, and Boston. He was born into a family that possessed not only the advantage of his father's reputation, but a genuine New England ancestry of ministers and merchants, and he married in 1862 the daughter of a wealthy and socially prominent Boston family. His career as a Harvard undergraduate was mediocre (he stood 71st in a class of 91), but he recouped with a quick M.A. and a B.Sc. in chemistry, *summa cum laude*, in 1863.[22]

In the beginning these kinds of unchallengable marks of identity paid off well. During two years in the late 1860s, he was invited to give lectures at Harvard, though he was not made a member of the faculty proper. Under his father's auspices he was given important work in the United States Coast Survey, but then, in the 1870s, things began to go badly. Peirce was not offered a permanent place at Harvard, and he could not get a teaching job at another college or university. In 1875, while he was in Europe doing experiments for the Coast Survey, his wife left him, adding to a developing reputation for strangeness and unreliability. He spent a winter in Europe, dressing extravagantly and living high, but got into financial difficulties with the Survey. Then, in 1879, things looked up momentarily when he was offered a lectureship at the new Johns Hopkins University. But, the following year, he lost his father and protector, and three years later was fired from the Johns Hopkins. Meantime, he had gotten a formal divorce and married a French woman whose reputation was always uncertain. In 1887, with a little money he had inherited, he moved to Milford, Pennsylvania where he tried to maintain a large estate and house on funds that were at first insufficient and later almost nonexistent. In 1891 he was finally fired from his part-time position with the Coast Survey, and from then on he lived almost on charity, in utter poverty, forced to write to friends that there was no food in the house and that he would soon not be able to write because the ink was going to freeze in its well. From the time he went to Milford, his isolation from philosophers and intellectuals was almost complete. In

---

22 Brent, "A Study of the Life of Charles Sanders Peirce," ch. 2. For other biographical data on Peirce, see Paul Weiss, "Charles Sanders Peirce," *Dictionary of American Biography*, XIV (New York, 1934); Feibleman, *An Introduction to Peirce's Philosophy*, ch. 1; Murphey, *The Development of Peirce's Philosophy*, chs. 1, 4, and 14.

1902 he claimed to Mrs. William James that he had gone for a period of five months without talking to another person except his wife, and with her only during a few "chats."[23]

As a young man, before he began to write this record of failure, Peirce was preoccupied with the notion of being a "successful man," or, as he put it in high school and college essays, of "mastering one's own fortune." He wrote essays on the qualities of personality a successful man ought to have, essays in which words like "boldness," "genius" and "destiny" were pivotal. But these youthful hankerings after success were accompanied by an impatience with discipline that gave Peirce a reputation, from the time he was in his late twenties, for irresponsibility. He never located an institution within which "boldness" and "destiny" had any currency. Instead, his life was an affair of jobs picked up and laid down—decades of on-and-off work with the Coast Survey, temporary lectureships, a regular university job briefly held. Through it all, he was full of queer schemes for making reputation and fortune. He once tried to start a correspondence school of logic, which he promised himself would prove a "big thing." And in the mid-1890s when he could hardly pay simple expenses, he tried to join an electric-power investment pool which he supposed would make a fortune. Time and again, he proved the validity of his first wife's judgment, that he was given to "rushing things through with recklessness and extravagancy."[24]

Carelessness and extravagance were complicated by vague rumors of immorality, and more concrete suggestions of insanity followed Peirce from the 1860s on. At the very least, he seems to have been disagreeable. In college William James described him as "smart" but "pretty independent and violent." Henry James, who met Peirce several times in Paris, found him lacking in the "art of making himself agreeable." His second wife even claimed that Peirce beat her, and during the Milford years he was twice indicted for hitting other women. In the end even William James, who always admired Peirce publicly, refused to help him get a

---

[23] Peirce to Mrs. William James, April 12, 1902, in Ralph Barton Perry, *The Thought and Character of William James* (Two volumes. Boston, 1935), II, p. 423; Peirce to William James, June 13, 1907, quoted in Brent, "A Study of the Life of Charles Sanders Peirce," p. 133.
[24] Brent, "A Study of the Life of Charles Sanders Peirce," pp. 38-39, 114-115, 117, 146-147.

university appointment because of Peirce's "curious misanthropy" and his inability to *"make connection* with anyone he is with." To the career problems caused by this obvious disagreeableness, there was added the problem of the constant suspicion he was under. From the first, people suspected him of various things—drunkenness, dope addiction, homosexuality—and this sort of reputation still lingers around him. The president of the Johns Hopkins once refused to sleep in the same house with "so immoral a man." Peirce himself lent credence to rumor by frequently claiming to be on the verge of collapse or suicide. Almost annually, during his brief tenure at the Johns Hopkins, he either threatened to resign or failed to teach his classes giving the possibility of mental breakdown as his reason. Toward the end of his life he openly threatened to kill himself.[25]

All these difficulties, which would have been serious enough in any context, were made even more damaging by the kind of institutional world Peirce confronted in the 1870s and 1880s. It was no longer enough for the New England intellectual to "travel much in Concord," as Thoreau had put it. Most of the best minds of the generation left Cambridge, Boston, and Concord for new lives in Europe, New York, Washington, and on a multiplying number of university campuses scattered between Baltimore and San Francisco. Among the handful of really interesting thinkers who grew up around Boston, all but William James eventually made careers outside New England. The kinds of credentials with which Peirce came equipped might have enabled him to survive well in ante-bellum Cambridge, where even his peculiarities might have had a perverse value, but after the Civil War, local and regional culture took on a distinctly second-best quality. New Englanders joined Southerners and Midwesterners in a nationalized intellectual world, dominated for the first time by universities and the associated paraphernalia of organizations like the American Economic Association or the American Historical Association. It became increasingly imperative for a man to identify himself with a scholarly discipline and to join distant and

25 William James to his family, September 16, 1861, in Perry, *Thought and Character of William James,* I, p. 211; Henry James to William James, November 18, 1872, in *Ibid.,* I, pp. 361-362; William James to G. H. Howison, April 2, 1894, *Ibid.,* II, p. 117; Brent, "A Study of the Life of Charles Sanders Peirce," pp. 89-106, 133.

often unknown colleagues in an appropriate society. Except for
certain unassimilables (writers and artists, usually) American
thinkers progressively identified themselves with their universities
and their organized "subjects." Outside the university, the institutionalized discipline, and the professional association they risked
either a loss or a devaluation of the sorts of local identity that had
meant so much to Emerson and his friends and contemporaries.

One of the most striking features of this institutionalization of
intellect was the itineracy, both physical and intellectual, that it
encouraged. The typical career pattern of the intellectual of the
period involved several changes of university and perhaps as
many changes of discipline. This itineracy intensified the problem,
always difficult for the intellectual in America, of developing a
sense of just who he was and what role he filled. For Peirce the
difficulty was redoubled by the fact that he never attained even a
semipermanent place in this institutional world whose claims to
supremacy he recognized. He suffered through the itineracy but
got none of its rewards. He was a drifter in a world of itinerants,
a member of no concrete community at all. When William James
tried to salvage Peirce's career in the 1890s by naming him the
creator of pragmatism, it was too late. Peirce had set too firmly
in the mold of eccentricity, isolation, and loneliness. He committed himself philosophically to "community" in the 1860s. At
the outset, the commitment was a function of the kind of genteel,
Sabbath ethic in which his family was immersed. But, as he became progressively insulated from the men and institutions
around him, he became only more insistent on the community as
an ideal. An eerie dialogue developed between his career and his
philosophical stance. As he was shut out of one concrete community after another, he responded by proclaiming his essential
unity in love with infinite community as abstract, in the last resort,
as Emerson's Nature. Failure in the short run only produced a
more and more eloquent faith that in the infinitely long run *his*
community would succeed. The communities in which he failed
to find membership were finite, concrete, and organized. The concept of community with which he retorted to this experience was
infinite, ideal, and not bound up in any institution, present or
future.

The radical texture of Peirce's ethical demands, the declining trajectory of his career, and the eccentricities that shaded over into near madness all declared the same thing about his relationship with his society. He was an outcast, a role he both won and had forced upon himself. He chose to dramatize his alienated standing primarily around the cluster of cultural values that Thorstein Veblen called "pecuniary"—the practical, materially progressive, anti-idealistic mentality that Peirce and most of his contemporaries attributed to America in what some of them came to call the "Gilded Age." In fact the social attitudes of most Americans of the period were *not* simply pecuniary, but combined a devotion to practicality with an intense moralism and idealism. But for Peirce, and for other intellectuals who wanted to claim a separation from the culture at large, it was almost a stylistic ritual to berate American "civilization" for its worship of practical—that is, financial—success. Peirce adopted this injured manner with vigor, as well he might, even at times when he was trying to make financial coups for himself. He focused his attack on American life on the opposition between scientific truth and what was "practical." His "pragmatism" was not at all an affair of practicality in any customary sense, but a demanding idealism, and he filled his essays with increasingly bitter jibes at what he took to be the popular ideology of the period. "Though I do hail from New York," he wrote in 1898,

> I shall hardly be mistaken for a Wall Street Philistine. A useless inquiry, provided it is a systematic one, is pretty much the same thing as a scientific inquiry. Or, at any rate, if a scientific inquiry becomes by any mischance useful, that aspect of it has to be kept sedulously out of sight during the investigation, or else . . . its hopes of success are fatally cursed.[26]

His lectures and articles were laced with paradoxes on the nature of what was useful, practical, or "vitally important." The point, always, was that inquiry to be genuine must be ornamental, must have no real connection with motives of comfort and power. Genuine "practicality," he argued, could be achieved only by a complete subjection of such motives to the ideal interest and destiny of the community of inquiry.

The same kind of irony clothed Peirce's numerous references to

---

[26] "Detached Ideas on Vitally Important Topics," a lecture of 1898, *Collected Papers*, 1.668.

insurance companies. Every man, he thought, ought to behave like an insurance company with an infinite number of policy-holders (all other men) whose security he would jealously guard. Such a man would be a model member of the community and would act always in the community's interests. If every man regarded himself as an ethical insurance company, protecting all other men against loss, then the community would be realized. The irony lay in the fact, which Peirce knew full well, that the ethic of capitalism enjoined every man to play the role, not of company but of policyholder, to be interested only in his own security. He always claimed to fear and despise "the worship of business, the life in which the fertilizing stream of genial sentiment dries up or shrinks to a rill of comic tid-bits."[27]

Peirce's loyalty to the community, reinforced by his own failings, also set him against any kind of evolutionary interpretation of life as a competitive struggle for survival. Many other American intellectuals, men such as John Fiske, Henry George, or Lester Frank Ward, were as intent as Peirce on finding some kind of intellectual shield against the tooth and claw of Darwinian nature. Their usual tactic was to claim that man's social life allowed him to transcend his natural animality and to live by a higher set of ethical rules. As always, such a compromising tactic would not do for Peirce. He was so thoroughly out of sympathy with what he supposed was the general ethos of Darwinism that he could rest only with a thorough reinterpretation of evolution, a reinterpretation that would import humane ethics into the "tangled bank," as Darwin described organic nature.[28]

Peirce read the *Origin of Species* soon after its publication, and he often praised Darwin as a man of science. But one of the remarkable things about Peirce's intellectual development is the late date at which he actually came to full grips with the problem of evolution. He certainly could make no use of Darwinism, for it seemed to make thought a mere byproduct of evolution, a piece of random flotsam cast up by the tide of natural selection.

[27] "Grounds of Validity of the Laws of Logic," 5.354; "Doctrine of Chances," 2.653; "Detached Ideas on Vitally Important Topics," 1.673.
[28] On Peirce's evolutionary cosmogony, see Philip P. Wiener, *Evolution and the Founders of Pragmatism* (Cambridge, 1949), ch. 4; and Charles Hartshorne, "Charles Sanders Peirce's Metaphysics of Evolution," *New England Quarterly*, 14 (March, 1941), pp. 49-63.

For Peirce, on the other hand, the very life of man was thought. The organism, so far as it had any meaningful existence at all, was only an instrument of the intellect. The kind of "impractical" intellectual activity Peirce regarded as the chief end of man could not have been the fruit of natural selection:

> Logicality in regard to practical matters . . . might . . . result from natural selection; but outside of these it is probably of more advantage to the animal to have his mind filled with pleasing and encouraging visions, independently of their truth; and thus, upon impractical subjects, natural selection might occasion a fallacious tendency of thought.[29]

The social implications of Darwinism, especially as they were "deduced" by Spencer, seemed to Peirce deplorable. Until he could create a thoroughgoing evolutionary philosophy consonant with the gospel of love he preached, Peirce contented himself with a few scattered references to Darwin and Spencer.[30]

His intellectual dilemma was acute. He could neither live successfully in the America of industrial capitalism, nor accept most of the ideas that bubbled endlessly out of the evolutionary fountain. To keep the two sides of his life in even the most primitive harmony, Peirce had to assiduously protect them both from the inroads of what he took to be social realities, on the one side, and from theories of competitive struggle, on the other. His central ethical ideal, the community of love, enabled him to rationalize his failure to achieve concrete membership in actually existing communities. It also provided him with a grounding for a carefully constructed philosophy, which might crumble if undermined by narrowly construed Darwinian concepts. For Peirce, no gentle accommodation either to the worship of business or to the tangled bank was possible. He was a logician, who placed a high value on scientific cool-headedness. But the precariousness

---

[29] "The Fixation of Belief," 5.366. In 1903 Peirce appended a note to this passage further qualifying his acceptance of Darwinism: "Let us not, however, be cocksure that natural selection is the only factor of evolution; and until this momentous proposition has been much better proved than as yet it has been, let it not blind us to the force [of] very sound reasoning."

[30] Peirce described "Spencerism" as "amateurism." Spencer, he thought, was "absurd . . . a man who will talk pretentiously of what he knows nothing about." "The Bedrock Beneath Pragmaticism," a fragment of 1906, in *Collected Papers*, 6.175; "Science and Immortality," a paper in a symposium published in the *Christian Register* of Boston in 1887, in *Collected Papers*, 6.554.

of his position finally forced him to boil over in a violent, impassioned denunciation of industrial society and evolutionary ethics. The fruit was a series of essays, published in *The Monist* in 1891-1893, flights of imagination not very becoming to a logician but containing some of the most remarkably humane and spirited language ever set down by an American.

The climax of the *Monist series* was Peirce's essay on "Evolutionary Love," in which he struck out at both the theory and practice of the Gilded Age. The cardinal fact about the nineteenth century, Peirce claimed, was its "unlovely hardness," its insensitivity to pain. This insensitivity, possibly the result of the introduction of anesthetics and the consequent loss of direct acquaintance with suffering, inclined the century to "relish a ruthless theory." As so it did, both in social practice and scientific theory. Thirty years after his Cambridge oration, Peirce was still condemning the Present Age for its lack of love. But frustration and failure had taken their toll, and he was no longer sanguine about how the Age would die:

> Soon a flash and quick peal will shake economists quite out of their complacency, too late. The twentieth century, in its latter half, shall surely see the deluge-tempest burst upon the social order—to clear a world as deep in ruin as that greed-philosophy has long plunged it into guilt.

The dominant and intimately related facts about the nineteenth century, in Peirce's mind, were capitalism and Darwinism. In its political economy and its evolutionary theory the century had committed itself to a gospel of greed, perfectly at odds with the gospel of love Peirce always preached. The formula of redemption of political economy was that "Intelligence in the service of greed ensures the justest prices, the fairest dealings between men, and leads to . . . food in plenty and perfect comfort." The social teaching and practice of the century were, Peirce claimed, summed up in the dictum that "greed is the great agent in the elevation of the universe." According to this blasphemy against the gospel of love, every "Wall street sharp," every "millionaire Master in glomery" was a "good angel," every miser a "beneficent power in a community."[31]

Of course, Peirce acknowledged, the ministers of the gospel of

---

[31] "Evolutionary Love," *The Monist* (1893), in *Collected Papers*, 6.287-295.

greed usually disguised their message with some euphemism, such as "love of self." They usually called upon the almighty as a justification and source for their ethic, flavored their Mammon with a *soupcon* of God. But no euphemism or theological sophistry could disguise the horror of the "atrocious villainies" of the apologists for industrial capitalism. They were only trying to excuse the man "who takes money from heedless persons not likely to guard it properly, who wrecks feeble enterprises better stopped, and who administers wholesome lessons to unwary scientific men by passing worthless checks upon them."[32]

Darwinism, Peirce claimed, was merely an extension into biology of the political economy of capitalism. Had Darwin been as good an intellectual historian as he was a naturalist, he might have had the presence of mind to place the motto of the gospel of greed on his title page: "Every individual for himself, and the Devil take the hindmost!" Darwin's analysis of natural selection was among the most "ingenious" and "pretty" scientific hypotheses ever devised, but it was far from proved. Its incredible popularity could be accounted for only by the fact that it was so perfectly consonant with the theory and practice of capitalism. Darwinism, no less than political economy, "made the felicity of the lambs just the damnation of the goats."[33]

By the 1890s most American theologians of any intellectual consequence had achieved one or another kind of accommodation with Darwinism. Peirce believed that such an accommodation was possible only within a grim and essentially un-Christian reading of the New Testament. Darwinism, as an interpretation of creation, was consistent only with the bitter, aberrant spirit of the Scribe of the Apocalypse, "stung at length by persecution into a rage, unable to distinguish suggestions of evil from visions of heaven . . . the Slanderer of God to men." The elements of struggle and death that provided the propelling force of Darwinian evolu-

---

[32] *Ibid.*, 6.292. The example of political economy Peirce chose to vilify, without naming it, was Simon Newcomb's *Principles of Political Economy* (New York, 1886). Newcomb had been instrumental in Peirce's dismissal from Johns Hopkins and had also played a part in Peirce's dismissal from the Coast Survey. It is obvious that Peirce's condemnation of the gospel of greed, the Wall Street sharp, the master of glomery was an exercise in revenge.

[33] *Ibid.*, 6.293, 297, 304.

tion could be fitted into only a harsh, hyper-Calvinist interpretation of Christianity, and in Peirce's eyes such a rendering of Christianity was a blasphemy against the Holy Ghost, whose essence was love. Darwinian Christianity could have as its message only the dire and unlovely theme that "all the time Christ was talking about having come to save the world, the secret design was to catch the entire human race, with the exception of a paltry 144,000, and souse them all in a brimstone lake."[34]

Peirce set himself the task of composing a theory of evolution consistent with his own kindly interpretation of Christianity and consonant with the ideal of community. As a model, he chose Lamarck's hypothesis that variations within species were the result of the transmission from generation to generation of acquired characteristics. In the Darwinian view, variation was conceived as strictly a matter of chance—the environment rigidly selected some chance variations and ruthlessly killed off the remainder. The Lamarckian model, however, left room for purposive behavior on the part of individual organisms. Hence Lamarck's hypothesis, though rejected by most American and European biologists by 1890, could be made to fit in with Peirce's broadly teleological view of the universe. "To say that the future does not influence the present is untenable doctrine. It is as much as to say that there are no final causes, or ends. The organic world is full of refutations of that position. Such action constitutes evolution."[35]

Peirce interpreted the Lamarckian process as an organic manifestation of the selfless love that made the community of inquiry possible. If variation depended on purposive behavior, he argued, then each organism, by seeking to acquire useful habits, sought not merely its own survival, but the survival of its species at large. Each organism, Peirce thought, acted consistently with the central dictum of Peirce's reading of the gospel of Christ: "progress comes from every individual merging his individuality in sympathy with his neighbors." In Peirce's imaginative rendering of the Lamarckian theory, no organism acted selfishly in its own interest. Every organism, including man, fulfilled the requirements of the Pauline ethic of faith, hope, and charity.[36]

[34] "Evolutionary Love," 6.287, 311.
[35] "Partial Synopsis of a Proposed Work in Logic," c. 1902, in *Collected Papers*, 2.86.
[36] "Evolutionary Love," 6.296-305.

In his discussion of evolution, as in all the parts of his philosophy that dealt with community, Peirce was radical. He posed no intermediate questions and returned no intermediate answers. He set an absolute choice between the individual and the community, and there was nowhere in his work any suggestion of a bargain, of a manipulated harmony. It is tempting, always, to set such a radical thinker apart from his age, to conclude that he stood somehow outside the main current of intellectual history. This was, in fact, the way Peirce saw himself. "Nobody understands me," he wrote to William James in 1907. "America is no place for such as I am."[37] It is even easier (and more frequently done) to ignore the radicalism, to seize on certain mere facets of Peirce's philosophy, to make him the "father" of pragmatism or a "forerunner" of twentieth-century positivism. But either setting Peirce entirely apart, or fitting him into this or that philosophical school, ignores his most instructive importance. His critique of individualism and his assertion of the ideal of community were the extreme formulation of the characteristic themes of the period, responses to the same challenges—Darwinism, industrial capitalism, and difficulties of career—which controlled the intellectual lives of the best of the intellectuals who were his contemporaries. Peirce had the most rigidly logical mind of his century, and it was combined with the rawest kind of sensitivity, so his responses were bound to be immoderate. But if he was radical, he was only a radical spokesman for his generation of intellectuals. His themes are muted in other writers, confused by lingering attachment to the slogans of individualism, but they are still the same themes.

---

[37] Peirce to James, June 13, 1907, quoted in Brent, "A Study of the Life of Charles Sanders Peirce," p. 133.

Chapter 3

James Mark Baldwin: Conservator of Moral Community

James Mark Baldwin, living in Paris after the Great War and reminiscing about a career that had ended, mused over what seemed to him a paradox in the architecture of his old school, Princeton. The university buildings were dignified and harmonious (even his sensitive French friends were impressed when they visited the campus), but there was something vaguely discomforting about the Gothic style. Dark, restrictive windows, anachronisms harking back to narrow Scholastic doctrine, seemed to shut light out of rooms where enlightenment ought to be at a premium. In Oxford the paradox might not have been so striking, for there a scholar unable to see his text had only to close his eyes and "let the ambient air of tradition and historical culture flow into his soul!" But let the Princeton student (or any other American scholar) appear to muse in the dim light, and the result would be an immediate reproof for idleness and the presentation of a petition for high-powered electric light to break "the charm of Gothic gloom."[1]

In this casual rumination, written when he was in his sixties, Baldwin summed up in metaphor his own intellectual career. Both "historical culture" and the progress symbolized by electric light exercised a compelling attraction, and he set himself the

[1] James Mark Baldwin, *Between Two Wars, 1861-1921, Memories, Opinions and Letters Received by James Mark Baldwin* (Two volumes, Boston, 1926), I, pp. 100-101.

intellectual task of discovering some kind of harmony between the past and the future, between ordered and stable tradition, on the one side, and advancing, inventive progress on the other. Like most of the other members of his generation, he was captured by the idea of progress, acutely aware of evolution, social change, and technological advance. Unlike many of his contemporaries, he was uneasy about casting off too lightly the burden of history and tradition. Baldwin was too progressive, in a broad and non-political sense, to be at home with the narrow spirit that dominated Princeton during his years there as a student and a teacher. But he was conservative enough to fear the prospect of a world without a firm and stable moral foundation. The fear of radical change in an anchorless society never was far from the surface of his scientific and didactic social psychology. The fear lurked behind his turgid, academic texts in vague and shifting forms— a dangerous criminal, a rampant mob, and, ultimate in dangers, the French Revolution.

The antinomy of tradition and progress was at bottom a question of morality. Baldwin's goal was a program of social change in which traditional morality would check and guide progress. The most important prerequisite for such a program was to discover a modern and scientific foundation for morality. Baldwin devoted himself to warding off social disintegration by finding scientific and progressive justifications for an inherited morality, thus equipping that morality to govern and control the future. His values, in the end, were those he learned in a strict, religious home and found confirmed at Princeton in the 1880s by James McCosh and other Presbyterian divines—moderation, conscience, duty, obligation, and moral striving. The specific content of conscience, the objects of duty and obligation, the exact nature of the "right," he always took for granted—honesty, industry, a decent respect for the rights and needs of others, a moderate charity, obedience to the law, these and other virtues which he tried, as a youth, to teach Sunday school classes and YMCA meetings. He sought new sanctions for this morality in the new evolutionary and experimental psychology and sociology in an effort to avoid a drastic and violent confrontation between a moral *ancien régime* and an amoral revolution.

Baldwin read the Civil War and reconstruction as an early lesson in the dangers of conflict between inflexible tradition and radical change. He was born in Columbia, South Carolina in 1861 and witnessed the burning of Columbia by Sherman's troops and what his family regarded as the villainies of black reconstruction. The die-hard Southerners, the "fire-eating parsons," and the "sweet but determined women" represented to him the dangers of a fixed tradition, unwilling to look change in the eye. The abolitionists and the black legislators, on the other side, were just as dangerous, for they threw off too easily the burdens of tradition and threatened chaos and anarchy. Baldwin was just a boy during the war and reconstruction, but he absorbed from his family a strong distaste for the excesses of either side, and he spent his academic life seeking a safe, sound middle ground, an intellectual vantage from which he could choose among the virtues of both the past and the future and avoid the evils of each.[2] As a youth, Baldwin felt a "call" to the ministry, and, against the day when he might mount to his pulpit, he "worked" in the Columbia YMCA and helped conduct Sunday services in the nearby penitentiary. When Baldwin was twenty, in 1881, he enrolled in the College of New Jersey to prepare for the ministry. The strongest intellectual influence at Princeton was the venerable President, McCosh, America's most prolific exponent of Scottish "common-sense" realism. In his intellectual career Baldwin made little or no use of the technical details of Scottish realism, but he never departed from its central ethical doctrine—that man is a free and responsible moral agent, bound by conscience to discover and do the right, and accountable to God for his actions.[3]

McCosh confirmed Baldwin in the faith that the universe is fundamentally moral, guided, albeit in mysterious ways, by Providence. In his maturity Baldwin rejected the doctrinal tenets of Presbyterian Christianity, but he never surrendered his faith in the intimate connection between the natural and the moral, sci-

[2] *Between Two Wars,* I, pp. 5-10.
[3] *The Life of James McCosh, A Record Chiefly Autobiographical,* William Milligan Sloane, ed. (New York, 1896), chs. 12-16; *Between Two Wars,* I, ch. 2; selected letters of McCosh to Baldwin are in *Ibid.,* II, pp. 199-203.

ence and ethics, the true and the good. McCosh taught him that science and religion revealed different aspects of the same divine truth and must, in the end, be compatible.[4] When Baldwin turned to the science of society, he clung to this belief. For him, to describe normal, unperverted social practice was also to prescribe ethical behavior. The quest for the ethical was identified with the discovery of what was biologically, psychologically, and socially natural.

McCosh also exemplified to Baldwin a sane, sound, and progressive conservatism. McCosh was the kind of conservative who kept a sharp eye on the enemy and on the future. He knew that to resist change, to fall into any kind of radicalism, even a radical conservatism, was to invite disaster. He was a staunch Republican, but he labored mightily to form a Civil Service Reform group on the Princeton campus. He realized the hopelessness of any unbending stance in the conflict between science and religion and led the way toward a reconciliation of Darwinism and conservative theology. It was in McCosh's classes, and not through any infidel philosopher, that Baldwin first encountered *The Origin of Species* and the experimental psychology of Wilhelm Wundt. Later, when Baldwin forsook the ministry for scientific psychology and evolutionary sociology, he could do so without suffering any intellectual trauma or feeling that the moral foundations of his life were being challenged in any fundamental way.[5]

Baldwin went to Germany after graduation from Princeton, carrying with him McCosh's mandate to learn all he could but to "keep your own faith in the most irreligious country I ever visited." The warning was unnecessary. Baldwin spent a quick year in Germany, jumping from one university to another. At Leipsig he listened to a few of Wundt's lectures but served mainly as a subject in the experiments of the more advanced students. He read some Spinoza, traveled around Germany a bit, and then

---

[4] When he retired from Princeton in 1888, McCosh summed up his attitude toward science: "I believe that whatever supposed discrepancies may come up for a time between science and revealed truth will soon disappear, that each will confirm the other, and both will tend to promote the glory of God." *The Life of James McCosh*, Sloane, ed., pp. 234-235.
[5] *Ibid.*, Sloane, ed., p. 258; *Between Two Wars*, I, pp. 20-21.

came home again to Princeton. Baldwin read fairly extensively in German psychology from time to time in his career, but he very often found relief in French discussions of German thought. His first book-length publication when he returned to the United States was a translation of Theodule Ribot's *German Psychology of Today*. In articles, published mainly in Presbyterian journals in the late 1880s, Baldwin mechanically recounted the new measuring techniques of the Germans and in the early 1890s engaged in some laboratory work himself. But, like William James and G. Stanley Hall, he became increasingly dissatisfied with "brass instrument" psychology. His bent toward moral philosophy was too strong to allow him to while away his life in a laboratory, laboriously measuring reaction times and optical illusions. He aways tried to give his social psychology an aura of laboratory reliability, inserting tables of observations here and there, but his principal concern was with moral, not experimental problems.[6]

After his return from Germany, Baldwin was engaged by Princeton as instructor in French and German—subjects for which he had no particular affection or talent. He enrolled in Princeton Theological Seminary, but his determination to enter the ministry gradually waned until he decided instead to make an academic career in psychology. This decision was not an intellectual about-face, nor was it the result of any great amount of doubting and soul-searching. Baldwin gradually and almost imperceptibly abandoned the ritualistic and supernatural elements of Christianity but remained committed to a belief in God and to the moral and social teachings of Protestant Christianity. Like dozens of other American intellectuals who chose academic careers during the period, Baldwin thought of the university as only a new institution, more effective than churches, for promoting morality.

Baldwin took his first teaching job at Lake Forest University in Illinois in 1887. The school specialized in training candidates for the ministry and missionary work in China. It was a stronghold of tradition, and Baldwin was extremely unhappy during his two years there. Hoping for promotion to a better school, he got

---

[6] *Between Two Wars*, I, pp. 31-32, 39, II, pp. 199-200, a good selection of Baldwin's work in labo.atory psychology is reprinted in *Fragments in Philosophy and Science, being Collected Essays and Addresses by James Mark Baldwin* (New York, 1902), chs. 13-18.

together the first volume of a *Handbook of Psychology*. Fortune smiled, and he was called to Toronto to a chair of metaphysics and logic. There he set up what he claimed was the first psychological laboratory anywhere on British soil and worked out a number of experiments, Germanic in their thoroughness and exactitude but little concerned with the social and moral problems that most disturbed him. After he left Toronto for Princeton in 1893 and during his last regular academic job at Johns Hopkins after the turn of the century, Baldwin's involvement in laboratory psychology became steadily more tenuous, until finally he deserted the laboratory altogether for social philosophy.[7]

The difficulty with mere experimental and physiological psychology, from Baldwin's point of view, was that it had little or no bearing on men's conduct in the world of moral dilemma and decision. Psychology had the advantage over theology because it was scientific, but it could not satisfy his quest for a science of morality. Baldwin's great fear, as he said in his inaugural address at Toronto in 1890, was that morality might crumble for the lack of firm intellectual foundations. Society depended, in his eyes, on moral conscience. If the authority of conscience were removed, if "altruism and reciprocity of obligation and duty" were reduced by critics to mere convention, then every man would become an anarchist and a political libertine. Moral scepticism could lead only to the disintergration of society, "to the brink of the French Revolution—of the social disintegration due to Individualism in philosophy."[8]

This was the intellectual challenge that pressed in on Baldwin during the period of startling and disruptive social and intellectual change between the 1890s and the Great War. He had to defend against scepticism by providing an authoritative basis for social morality, to ward off the disintegration of society and the ethical caprice he associated with individualism. On the other side, however, he had to avoid the problems posed by an excessive collectivism, the tyranny of unbending moral authority he

---

[7] *Between Two Wars*, I, chs. 4-7.
[8] "Philosophy: Its Relation to Life and Education," *Fragments in Philosophy and Science*, pp. 8-9.

had witnessed at Lake Forest, or, even more frightening, the collective tyranny of the mob, of democracy run riot. Perverted individualism resulted in disintegration and chaos, but perverted collectivism led only to the other evil extreme, the loss of individual moral freedom and, hence, moral responsibility. The informing atmosphere of Baldwin's work is one of fear, fear of excesses in licentious individualism or of stultifying collectivism.

The problem of morality, of the antinomy of tradition and progress, thus resolved itself into the problem of striking a balance between individualism and collectivism, of finding a basis for the harmony of the private, individual self and the social group. As the mottoes for his most important and successful text, Baldwin chose St. Luke's "Thou shalt love thy neighbor as thyself," and two lines from Schiller,

> Strive to be whole, and if thou lackest the power, Be part of a whole and serve it with faithful heart.[9]

Apart from society, the individual could have no morality. "Morally," Baldwin concluded his first book on social psychology, "I am as much a part of society as physically I am a part of the world's fauna; and as my body gets its best explanation from the point of view of its place in the zoological scale, so morally I occupy a place in the social order."[10] Sin itself was a function of the social situation; without the prospect of being found out and chastised by the community a man could have no sense of guilt, no moral conscience. It was the project of teaching men to love their neighbor, to be part of a whole, that made Baldwin a social psychologist. This didactic project shaped his intellectual career, and the execution of it brought him a brief but meteoric academic fame.

Baldwin's intellectual style was very different from Peirce's. Indeed the contrast between the two men at almost every level is nearly complete. They had, however, one thing in common; they both realized early that the individual offered no solution. In company with other men as disparate as Josiah Royce, Herbert Croly, John Dewey, and G. Stanley Hall, Peirce and Baldwin

---

[9] *Social and Ethical Interpretations in Mental Development: A Study in Social Psychology* (New York, 1897), pp. 5, 447.
[10] *Mental Development in the Child and the Race* (New York, 1895), p. 488.

began with the primary assumption that a man is defined by his relations with other men and that whatever a man can or should become depends on his membership in a functioning community. Peirce's formal goal was truth; Baldwin's was morality. For both, however, the key to success lay in the existence of a proper community.

Peirce's solution to the problem of individuality and community never gained popularity among his contemporaries. It was too drastic, too technically perfect. The choice he posed was too stark—the individual, with all his peculiar emotions, desires, idiosyncracies, against the community and the pursuit of truth. Peirce left no room for compromise, no possibility that both the individual and the community might be justified. He demanded the complete sacrifice of the individual, and he made the demand not in the name of any concrete, realizable human end but in the name of an ideal, unembellished truth. In one sense Peirce was one of the most humane men of his or any other generation. He valued love almost as much as he did truth and rejected Darwinian evolutionary theory on the remarkably unscientific grounds that it was unlovely. But his ideal of love was shorn of familiar sentimental or emotional meanings. He called on men to make the commitment of Gethsemane; he asked them to rejoice in something utterly objective and unrelated to their own personal desires or fulfillment. Few men in any age have been willing to make such a commitment even in the name of a personal God, much less in the name of logic.

Baldwin gathered in the audience, the professorships, and titles which Peirce missed. For Baldwin provided what Peirce did not, an analysis of society in which both the individual and the group seemed to find justification. Whereas Peirce ignored wholesome social order and stability, Baldwin valiantly preserved them from sceptics and challengers. Perhaps most important, Baldwin was a thoroughgoing evolutionist. Peirce, during most of his career, did not use evolution as a sanction for community. He attempted to create community out of nothing by a kind of logical evangelism. Baldwin, on the other hand, made every possible use of evolution. His method was, through and through, genetic. He made copious use of every available European and American writer in the fields of evolutionary biology, psychology, anthropology, and sociology.

His social theory had the appearance, at least, of providing a rounded and comfortable synthesis of all the prestigious sciences of origin. The synthesis did not last, and Baldwin's reputation was short-lived. Peirce was an innovator and enjoyed a considerable revival in the twentieth century. Baldwin wrote for the nineteenth.

Baldwin's approach to biological evolution was ambiguous. He was determined to show that man's social state was natural and not artificial in origin. At the same time, he was unwilling to reduce the social to the biological. The social community and its attendant morality must have the sanction of nature, without being subject to nature's unreflective determinism. Thus Baldwin was led to reject both the dominant nineteenth-century views of the relationship of evolution and ethics. He rejected Spencerian naturalism because it provided no higher arbiter of right then the mere facts of existence and survival at any evolutionary stage. Spencer, Baldwin felt, reduced man to the ethical status of a steam engine.[11] But Baldwin also rejected the alternative view, associated most closely with Huxley, that evolution and ethics are entirely separate matters and that the "moral sense" directly contravenes the struggle for existence, since it runs counter to the instincts of survival.[12]

Spencer and Huxley, and their followers, reached different conclusions, Baldwin thought, by beginning with the same basic error. They associated both ethics and the struggle for existence

---

[11] Baldwin's many criticisms of Spencer are scattered throughout his writings. On this particular point, see especially *Social and Ethical Interpretations*, pp. 305-309. See also, "Mr. Spencer's Philosophy" (1897), *Fragments in Philosophy and Science*, pp. 353-358. Baldwin thought the Spencerian web of analogies from human affairs to chemistry and biology was "like proving a bed of tulips to be onions by . . . nipping off the tell-tale blooms."

[12] On Huxley, see Baldwin, *Development and Evolution, Psychophysical Evolution, Evolution by Orthoplasy, and the Theory of Genetic Modes* (New York, 1902), p. 283, and *Darwin and the Humanities* (Baltimore, 1909), ch. 3. The most extreme form of the separation of evolution and ethics Baldwin encountered was Benjamin Kidd's *Social Evolution* (New York, 1894). Kidd denied the possibility of any natural, rational sanctions for moral life and urged a flight into irrational religion to save society. Baldwin rejected Kidd out of hand, of course, arguing that the social impulse was natural and rational and that religion, as an expression of the social impluse, was just as natural and rational. *Social and Ethical Interpretations*, pp. 88-89. Cf. Richard Hofstadter, *Social Darwinism in American Thought* (Rev. ed., Boston, 1955), ch. 5.

with individuals. But with men, as with some of the higher animals, the unit of struggle was not the individual but the social group. "Morality has arisen because it is socially useful. . . . The preservation of a group depends on the character of its inner organization. This requires . . . the subordination and regulation of the individuals." The bridge between evolution and ethics, for Baldwin, was the social community. Social morality was a natural evolutionary phenomenon and not, as Huxley claimed, an artificial construction. But society, when it was truly human and reflective, also protected man from the nonmoral determinism of biology by providing him with higher ethical sanctions than those of individual survival. In the social community standards of "group utility" replaced those of "biological and individual utility." "The norms of social utility become the ideals of personal duty, which are unconditionally imperative to the individual."[13]

Baldwin constantly took advantage of the intellectual prestige of evolution and used it as a buttress for his social ethics, but he carefully skirted the limiting aspects of biology. He agreed with Spencer that "There is only one evolution." But the one evolution, he urged, had two sides, biological and psychological. Man might be, in part, the product of biology, but he transcended biology. Reflective and ethical society was not possible without the long preparation of biological ascent from the protozoan, but neither could society be understood through the microscope. Each individual man, Baldwin believed, recapitulated the evolutionary history of the race. He passed through, in abbreviated and imprecise stages, the stages of animal development his ancestors had traversed during the long evolutionary climb. But, like his ancestors, man passed finally out of the animal kingdom into a preeminently ethical kingdom of man, society.[14]

---

[13] Baldwin rejected the argument, which he associated with Kant, that the individual's ideas of personal duty were derived from what he privately determined was "fit" to be universal law. Baldwin wanted to avoid such a direct confrontation between man the cosmos, and he used society as a buffer. For Kant's rule, "So act that the principle of your conduct may be fit for universal law," Baldwin wanted to substitute, "So act that all the members of the social group . . . may know your conduct without pain to yourself." *Social and Ethical Interpretations,* p. 557; *Darwin and the Humanities,* pp. 62, 65-66.

[14] The notion of recapitulation, biological and cultural, recurs frequently in Baldwin's works. See particularly, *Mental Development,* pp. 1-36; *Social*

Along the route, each human infant inherited and developed characteristics that he shared with the lower animals—physical attributes, certain tendencies to instinctive emotion, such as bashfulness, and above all, the tendency to learn, to imitate, and to develop habits. At birth, Baldwin thought, the infant was distinguished from the animal principally by the extent of this imitative learning capacity.[15] Plasticity, the ability to accommodate, distinguished man from the animals. An animal might be eminently intelligent and even social, like the bee, and still not be capable of reflective and ethical behavior. The social insect, magnificently outfitted by nature at birth, was incapable of any significant learning, and the ability to learn by imitation and invention was for Baldwin the hallmark of true, human sociality. The human infant, in contrast to the insect and to most other animals, came into the world utterly helpless, a "bare naked presence . . . endowed only with what he had inherited, together with the magnificent capacity . . . of learning by the absorption of the social 'copy,' and of gradually growing into conformity to this copy both in his thought and in his conduct."[16]

In the overriding plasticity of man lay the secret of his learning to be social and, at the same time, retaining individuality. Because he was plastic, man could develop social habits and traditions and still keep the possibility of progress through innovation. Important as plasticity was to Baldwin, however, it was an insufficient key to the development of an ethical social community. On the criterion of plasticity alone, the difference between man and animal was a difference of degree. But ethical behavior, Baldwin

---

and Ethical Interpretations, pp. 189-193; *Development and Evolution,* pp. 1-21. The best available study of the recapitulation idea in American thought is Charles E. Strickland, "The Child and the Race" (Unpublished doctoral dissertation, University of Wisconsin, 1962).

[15] *Mental Development,* chs. 9-10.

[16] *Social and Ethical Interpretations,* pp. 58-59. In his use of imitation as a crucial process in social development, Baldwin paralleled closely the work of the French sociologist, Gabriel Tarde. He frequently acknowledged Tarde's work but claimed to have arrived at his own views independently. *Ibid., viii; Between Two Wars,* I, p. 68. On Tarde and Baldwin, see also Michael M. Davis, *Psychological Interpretations of Society (Studies in History, Economics and Public Law,* Columbia University, XXXIII, New York, 1909), and Fay Berger Karpf, *American Social Psychology, Its Origins, Development, and European Background* (New York, 1932), pp. 93-107, 269-276.

thought, was entirely peculiar to man. There had to be something peculiar to man, something to mark him off from animals, some faculty or power that was natural in its origin but transcended biology.

Following McCosh and the moral philosophers of the preceding generation, Baldwin found this distinctively human trait in reflective self-consciousness. No animal was self-conscious, but every man was. Self-consciousness made it possible for man to be ethical, to have ideals, to escape the mere physical influences of both heredity and environment. Only after the development of self-consciousness did man become a true moral agent, capable of self-denial, social continence and cooperation. But, unlike the traditional moral philosophers, Baldwin treated self-consciousness as a social outcome. He devised an elaborate "dialectic of personal growth" to account for the origin and nature of self-consciousness. This "dialectic" was the technical cornerstone of his social psychology, and it provided him with the basis for a theoretical reconciliation of the individual and the social community.[17]

Baldwin's dialectic of personal growth exemplified a pervasive tendency in the late nineteenth century to deny that self-consciousness was innate and intuitive, original in each individual man, something prior to, rather than gained from, experience.[18] Like Peirce, Baldwin maintained that the self, far from being private and purely personal, resulted from experience within a community of other selves. "It is impossible," Baldwin wrote, "for any one to begin life as an individualist in the sense of radically separating himself from his social fellows. The social bond is established and rooted in the very growth of self-consciousness."[19]

In earliest infancy, according to Baldwin, the child's world was

---

[17] *Mental Development*, pp. 300-301; for the dialectic of personal growth, see especially *Ibid.*, pp. 15-20; *Social and Ethical Interpretations*, pp. 7-56, and *The Individual and Society, or Psychology and Sociology* (Boston, 1911), pp. 13-32.

[18] The most significant American attempts to escape the tradition of a transcendent and inviolate personal soul or self were Peirce, "Questions Concerning Certain Faculties Claimed for Man" (1868), *Collected Papers*, 5.213-263; Chauncey Wright, The Evolution of Self-Consciousness" (1873), in *Philosophical Discussions*, Charles Eliot Norton, ed., (New York, 1877); William James, "The Consciousness of Self," *Principles of Psychology* (Two volumes, New York, 1890), I, ch. 10. Cf. Baldwin's review of James' *Principles* (1891), in *Fragments in Philosophy and Science*, pp. 371-389.

[19] *Individual and Society*, p. 26.

a world of pure perceptions, in which personal and impersonal objects were indistinguishable. Gradually, as he gained "cortical integration," the child learned to distinguish persons from objects. Parents, particularly, took on a special importance, and their activities were freighted with the most compelling kinds of consequences for the child. They became, what Baldwin called personal "projects" who set "copies" for imitation.

Repeated and continual efforts to imitate, accompanied by frequent failures, led the child to think of the "projects" as external. Thus the ego, the "subject" of experience, was born. This rudimentary idea of the self was the result of social encounter. The very conception of the subjective ego included the related idea of the projective alter. The child could not even think of himself and others separately, but could conceive of his self only as one pole of a social relationship.

The child, Baldwin claimed, "attributed" to his ego as subject the characteristics he observed in the alter as project. At the same time he encountered other persons, usually younger brothers or sisters, who were distinctly different from the parental projects. Unlike the parents, they did not impress their personalities on the child. In order to think of them as persons at all, he had to "eject" his own idea of himself onto them. By this process, the child created a new social relationship. He attributed to the "ejects" the qualities of his own subjective ego. They became the mirrors of his own self. The sense of self was an awareness of two social relationships. "The ego and the alter are thus born together. . . . My sense of yourself grows in terms of my sense of myself. Both ego and alter are thus essentially social. . . . The ego and the alter are to our thought one and the same thing."[20]

The two dominant instincts of living organisms, Baldwin thought, were the tendencies to habit and accommodation—thinly veiled biological analogues to tradition and progress in society. In the child's relations with his parents the tendency to natural and spontaneous accommodation held sway. Toward social ejects, on the other hand, he was habitual, selfish, and aggressive. Thus man had capacities for both generosity and selfishness. He was not innately good or evil, not a child of nature who was originally either noble and generous or brutish and selfish. He

---

[20] *Social and Ethical Interpretations,* pp. 9, 12.

was instead the generous imitator or the selfish bully and tyrant, depending on whether he encountered awesome projects or comprehensible ejects.[21]

At this level, the dialectic of personal growth and the resultant bipolar self were not ethical. Neither the accommodating nor the habitual self, taken alone, was capable of genuine moral acts. The accommodating self was capricious, too little restrained by inner compulsions. It was, if anything, too social and found its ultimate expression in mob violence. One of Baldwin's great fears was the mob—"a lynching party, a corn-riot, a commune, a Chamber of Deputies, or a Jingo Senate"— violent, capricious, casting tradition and law to the winds. Mobs allowed men to escape their "bondage to individualism" only to bend them to an equally onerous bondage to the rampant collective, the agency of disintegration in society and cataclysm in history.[22]

On the other side, however, the habitual self was too individualistic, too much rooted in private impulse, unsoftened by social sympathy, and unleavened by the potentiality of progress. The egoistic self of habit and aggression could protect man from the mere whim of social suggestion, but, alone, the habitual self was incapable of any kind of social morality. The accommodating self was the servant of caprice, and the habitual self the prisoner of constricting regularity. Separately, neither could be truly ethical. Baldwin created, out of whole cloth, an ethical "ideal self" which, he claimed, harmonized the lower selves of habit and accommodation.[23]

The ideal self was born, according to Baldwin's somewhat confused accounts, in situations in which the two lower selves came into direct conflict. When a child first became clearly aware (usually at about the age of three) of the simultaneous demands of these two selves, he took the first precarious step toward the development of an ethical ideal self. Most frequently, such encounters occurred when the father commanded the child to do something unpleasant. The habitual, selfish side of the child's personality resisted the command, and the accommodating

---

[21] *Social and Ethical Interpretations*, pp. 16-30.
[22] *Ibid.*, pp. 237-241.
[23] *Mental Development*, pp. 336-346; *Ibid.*, pp. 34-51. Baldwin had a great many reservations about Hegel, but he thought Hegel's account of the self was "altogether the best ever written." *Mental Development*, p. 346.

self, whose imitations had always been spontaneous and voluntary, could not prevail. Obedience to the command required the
generation of a new and different notion of the self. This was the
ideal self, vague and elusive at first, an idea of the self as obedient
to law, wilfully and even painfully subjugating private habit to
social demands for obedience.

The ideal self, like the rudimentary, nonethical self, was bipolar and developed dialectically. Projects, holding duty aloft as
an ideal, provided the copies for imitation. Parents, then teachers,
state, and church set progressively higher and more complex
ethical copies. "Society produces the individual, and informs him
in what *thus becomes for him his absolute duty.*" The authority
of the ethical projects was gradually transferred to the subjective
ego and became the adult "conscience," the "moral sense." The
ideal self which was embodied in conscience could never be
realized, but was always retreating before the advance of the
actually existing self. "It is not I, but I am to become it. . . . My
ethical insight must always find its profoundest expression in that
yearning which anticipates, but does not overtake, the ideal."[24]

The ideal self was then dialectically attributed to progressively
"wider and richer" ethical ejects—other children, schoolmates,
and, finally, society at large. As the projects posed ideals for the
ethical subject, the subject in turn demanded ethical behavior
from the ejects. The child, then the adult, groped his way toward
the conception of a morality common to all, a social ideal
obligating every member of the community. The fully developed
ethical self-consciousness bound the individual to the society by
a compulsion infinitely more telling than mere physical coercion.
The ideal self was a "sort of speaking social companion," a
"shadowy being," which could exact social cooperation from all
but the criminal and the insane.[25]

Baldwin's analysis of the self solved (to his own satisfaction,
at any rate) the nagging problem of conflict between the individual and the community. Between a normal, sane man and a
natural, healthy society, there could be no irreconcilable conflict,
but only a thriving, reciprocal harmony. Each man was the child
of his society, and a society was a happy family of its own chil-

---

[24] *Mental Development*, p. 345; *Darwin and the Humanities*, p. 66.
[25] *Social and Ethical Interpretations*, p. 50.

dren. The "hideous un-fact," erroneously presumed by the "ego-ists," the Spencers, the Comtes and the Hobbeses, was that the natural man was in chronic protest against society. "Man," Bald-win triumphantly concluded, "is not a person who stands up in his isolated majesty, meanness, passion, or humility, and sees, hits, worships, fights, or overcomes another man, who does the opposite things to him, each preserving his own isolated majesty, so that he can be considered a 'unit' for the compounding proc-esses of social speculation. On the contrary, a man is a social outcome rather than a social unit. He is always, in his greatest part, also someone else."[26]

The actual process by which a man became "someone else" depended, Baldwin realized, on the smooth functioning of social institutions—the school, the state with its paraphernalia of laws and tribunals, and the church. Every society, no matter how primitive, had to have some more or less formal arrangements for "socializing" the young, restraining the occasional anti-social recalcitrant, and inculcating reverence for the common ideals of the community. As a society progressed, the "psychical relations" among its members became stronger and less dependent on ex-ternal institutional reinforcement. In a society of highly developed, reflective, ethical selves, governments could be more democratic and resort less and less to constraint. Educational institutions could concentrate more and more on developing rather than restraining the individual, and religion could gradually free itself from animism and fear and appeal more and more to reason and esthetic sensibilities. But no society could ever be completely free of external, objective institutions to guarantee continuity and stability in morality, science, and art.[27]

---

[26] *Social and Ethical Interpretations,* p. 87. Compare Spencer: "Setting out, then, with this principle, that the properties of the units determine the properties of the aggregate, we conclude that there must be a Social Science expressing the relations between the two." *The Study of Sociology* (New York, 1893), p. 52.

[27] *Social and Ethical Interpretations,* chs. 9-10; *Individual and Society,* ch. 4; article "Psychology of Religion," in *Dictionary of Philosophy and Psycho-logy,* Baldwin, ed., (Three vols., New York, 1902), II, pp. 459-462. One of Baldwin's chief criticisms of Hegel was that he relied too much on con-straint and the State. Josiah Royce, Baldwin felt, had remedied this short-coming of Hegel, and Baldwin claimed to be in "fundamental agreement" with Royce. *Social and Ethical Interpretations,* viii, p. 505.

Institutions, in Baldwin's scheme, were essentially conserving devices devoted to maintaining already existing social relations. Progress could not originate in such institutions but had to come from the rare individual who was capable of a healthy, fruitful conflict with conservative institutions. Most of the members of any society, because of the way in which their social selves developed, could be counted on to be "conservative and less original," near perfect mirrors of the community at large. Occasionally, however, society produced an exceptional man, a genius. The genius was the prime mover of progress. By an inventive stroke in science, in technology, or in philosophy, the genius could redeem the community from the "hard and fast solidification" which would result from the unleavened conservatism of the majority.[28]

This analysis of invention and progress enabled Baldwin to escape, finally, from the Spencerian tyranny of deterministic biological evolution. Social progress, unlike biological progress, was "ideal." A man's chief "inheritance" from his species was not his body or even his physiological brain, but a body of tradition and an anatomy of harmonious "psychical relations" with his social fellows. The most important variations within the species of social man were not variations in physical constitution, but variations of ideas, inventions of mind. If they were socially useful, the inventions "survived" and were transmitted to the next social generation. If they had no adaptive value in the social environment, the inventions perished.[29]

Man remained tied to biological evolution only by what

---

[28] *Social and Ethical Interpretations*, chs. 3-5. Darwin, Baldwin thought, was the very type of a genius with a keenly developed "social judgement." The French Revolution exemplified to him the result of trying to impose a naked innovation, by fiat, on an unprepared society. *Darwin and the Humanities*, pp. 109-111.

[29] Baldwin cautiously maintained that the test of the truth of any idea was its social utility. The criteria of what was to be counted true knowledge were social and, generally speaking, instrumental; the truth was what was held in common. *Social and Ethical Interpretations*, pp. 97-125; *Thought and Things, A Study of the Development and Meaning of Thought, or Genetic Logic* (Three vols., New York, 1906-1911), I, ch. 8, and II, chs. 2, 9. Baldwin was sympathetic, with reservations, to his own understanding of pragmatism and instrumentalism. *Between Two Wars*, I, p. 123. "Its effects on life are, in a general way, and where historically interpreted, a legitimate test of the truth or falsity of a philosophical doctrine or system." "Philosophy: Its Relation to Life and Education" (1890), *Fragments in Philosophy and Science*, p. 9.

Baldwin called "extra-social factors—disease, which might take a genius before he could give his invention to the world; war, which was the most important surviving remnant of group struggle in the biological world; and the birth of children who were hereditarily unfit to become members of society. The effects of such "extra-social" limitations on the progress of the social community were constantly being reduced. Baldwin believed (before World War I, at least) that the development of international law and arbitration was bringing the elimination of war nearer and nearer. Medical science seemed to be winning for man a wider and wider circle of immunity from the perils of his environment and the weaknesses of his body.[30]

But society had thus far failed to exert any deliberate, reflective control over the most powerful extra-social restraint on progress, child-bearing. "It is the duty of each individual," Baldwin proclaimed, "to be born a man of the social tendencies which his communal tradition requires of him." To insure that every new member of society would be a man of "social tendencies," Baldwin advocated a program of eugenics to prevent the continued reproduction of socially unfit children. Surgical eugenics, he believed, would do more than any other reform to loose society from the chafing restraints of biology and give social selection full and free play.[31]

"Social selection" was thus the end result of man's tendencies to imitate and invent, tendencies just as natural to man as the breathing reflex. Baldwin admitted that in some areas, notably commerce, even the most advanced societies did not seem to have risen above the level of biological competition. But even commerce must eventually give way before the inevitable tendency "toward the complete regulation and use of the forces of the individual in the interests of social and ethical unity and co-operation."[32]

Baldwin's elaborate and somewhat confused vision of the ethical community enabled him to calm (temporarily, at least) his

[30] *Individual and Society,* pp. 162-170; "The Social and the Extra-Social," *American Journal of Sociology,* 4 (March, 1899), pp. 649-655.
[31] *Individual and Society,* pp. 169-170; *Social and Ethical Interpretations,* pp. 76-77.
[32] *Ibid.,* pp. 60-61, 462-465, 510-519.

bothersome doubts about the feasibility of a society that was at once stable and advancing. Above his tangled and querulous discussions of specific technical problems in biology and psychology, his theory of the social man appeared well-wrought and symmetrical. He justified both the individual and the community, resolved their conflicts, and made them subtly interdependent. He embedded the good society firmly within an evolutionary world view and still left man free to transcend his animality. He rescued tradition and institutions from the acid of undirected change by making them the indispensable filters through which any lasting and beneficial social advance must pass. He saved both history and progress by interpreting the past as the source and governor of the future. He gave progress a definite, confident direction, shaped by man himself and not by any forces outside the widening circle of human control. Though any society might temporarily violate its own best nature, it must eventually regain the safe and sure road toward a higher and more harmonious ethical community in which conflict and violence were quelled. In theory Baldwin was confident that man, not things, was in the saddle and that society was destined to a good end.

Baldwin's intellectual career is a clear-cut example of the way the two challenges of evolutionary ideas and concrete social change converged on the problem of individualism. The concept of ethical community was, for Baldwin, a buffer which could shield man from both amoral nature and from a society run riot with drastic change. At one stroke, Baldwin hoped to quiet his fear of both social unrest and the Spencerian mechanism. The theoretical social man, with his ideal self, was a sort of talisman designed to fend off threats to both sides of Baldwin's restive double consciousness.

Intellectually, Baldwin was set adrift early in his life from the stable moorings of Presbytarianism and McCosh's moral philosophy. This intellectual drift was complicated by the characteristic itineracy of Balwin's life as a late nineteenth-century academician. He had difficulty finding a satisfactory discipline and moved from university to university. The longest stable period in his academic life was a ten-year stay at Princeton. This career led him far from the safety of his home in a Southern town, a home where discipline was strict and morality presumed to be obvious. He learned to enjoy travel, Scotch whiskey, and golf. By the standards of his parents' home, he was a suspect wanderer with no calling. Such a personal and intellectual history cried out for some kind of compensatory unification and rationalization. During the 1890s, at least, the ideal of ethical community gave the appearance of meaningful integration to Baldwin's life. It at least gave him membership in a theoretical society where Christian virtues prevailed over Darwinian strengths and where local roots were replaced by a more abstract and ubiquitous loyalty.

The ironic outcome, however, was that Baldwin's painfully built social theory failed him. It worked well enough as an antidote to evolution, but it failed to provide him with an adequate sense of membership in American society. The theoretical confidence he staked on the social man and the ideal self was betrayed by events. After the turn of the century, almost every development, political, social or economic, Baldwin observed in the United States either repelled or frightened him. He concluded that the ethical community, capstone of his social thought, would not be built in America.

The widest rent in Baldwin's confidence was torn by Progressive politics. In a very vague way Baldwin was a progressive and a reformer; he believed in cosmic progress. But the kinds of concrete social and political reforms that occupied his contemporaries seemed to him to be dangerous aberrations. Grover Cleveland was Baldwin's ideal political leader, and measured against the sane, honest, cautious standard of Cleveland, the leaders of political progressivism were unscrupulous demagogues. Theodore Roosevelt was a man of shallow, unworkable, ill-considered schemes. The Republican "Insurgents" in Congress were so dangerously insincere that they "chilled the moral heart of the nation." Of Wilson's "new freedom," Baldwin could only ask "What is it?" He had despised Wilson at Princeton and always thought him a man of arrogance and "slackness of ethical fibre," far "a-sea from the blessed islands of Decision" which had been plotted on the moral map by men of Cleveland's caliber.[33]

A review of American politics after the turn of the century forced Baldwin to a dismal conclusion: "Progress in matters social

---

[33] *Between Two Wars,* I, pp. 59-61, 98-99, 207-211, 275; "French and American Ideals" (1913), in *Ibid.,* II, pp. 5-6.

and ethical is being made, not because but in spite of the so-
called progressives, of whatever party, who bring forward half-
baked schemes of reform!" The half-baked schemes were just as
dangerous as the leaders. The prospect that judicial decisions
might become subject to recall terrified Baldwin. "Think of the
weapon this gives to the political trickster and moral mountebank
to work disorder and confusion while invoking the name of
'progress'. . . . There are in the world some constitutions that
cannot be revised, some decrees that cannot be annulled, some
judgements that cannot be recalled."[34]

Baldwin's basic fear of political progressivism was that it might
degenerate into mob action. He always paid lip service to democracy, but he profoundly distrusted the common man. In America, especially, he thought the plain man was too easily duped by
demagogues, too subject to social suggestion, too little individualized by the habitual and aggressive self. The Americans might be
competitive and individualistic in commerce, but Baldwin believed that in matters of style and morals they were all too anxious
to repress and stifle individuality. Americans believed too thoroughly in democracy, put too much faith in the judgment of the
average man. They even thought they could export democracy
immediately to any country. On visits to Mexico in the first decade of the twentieth century, Baldwin was highly impressed by
the "benign and healthful reign" of Porfirio Diaz. Diaz might be a
dictator and a tyrant, but he created the necessary political stability in which genuine progress was possible. Wilson, and by implication, America, talked foolishly of giving the Mexicans "liberty"
and the franchise, apparently forgetful of the "results of giving
the ballot to the intellectually and morally incompetent" during
the period of Reconstruction. "The more or less barbarous
hordes," Baldwin thought, "must work gradually into the new
freedom which rests on self-government and social continence."[35]

Conservatism in America seemed to Baldwin to be just as aberrant as the forces of reform or revolution. The Republican party

[34] "French and American Ideals," *Between Two Wars*, II, p. 11.
[35] "French Liberty and American" (1923), in *Between Two Wars*, II, pp.
138-147; *Ibid.*, I, pp. 131-134, 138, 157-158; "Mexico," *Nation*, 82(March,
1906), pp. 173-174; *American Neutrality, Its Cause and Cure* (New York,
1916), p. 24.

represented only capitalism, bureaucracy, special privilege, and territorial expansion. In matters of morals American conservatism was expressed in a stifling Puritanism. Progressivism perversely combined social caprice with an attempt to stifle individuality in economics, but conservative opinion was just as perverse a combination of "the strictest possible moral and social censorship" and "an unheard-of industrial license." Both of America's national selves, the accommodating, social self and the aggressive self of ego and habit, had somehow veered from their proper lines of development. The national self of generous accommodation was corrupted into mediocrity and a docile susceptibility to demagogic leaders. The national self of habit and aggression, instead of producing inventive geniuses and great leaders, produced only insincere politicians and "industrial kings." America had failed to generate a strong enough ideal self to bind these two lower, aberrant sides of its national personality together and lift them into a higher harmony.[36]

Baldwin had great hopes for both his social philosophy and his country. He never recanted any item of his social theory, and, even when he was most dissatisfied with his country, he staunchly called himself a thorough "Anglo-Saxon American." But his continual discovery of disagreement between the theoretical possibilities suggested by his social philosophy and the realities of his country led him to desert both. After 1900, he ignored social psychology in favor of metaphysics, and he left America for Europe. He became an ardent, if not entirely competent, metaphysician and a Frenchman in all but name.

Baldwin's intellectual career followed a predictable, almost straight ascending line from the narrow details of laboratory physiology and psychology, through evolutionary theory and social psychology, into metaphysics. He concluded with a vague cosmology of emergence, somewhat similar to Bergson's, and an esthetic theory of reality. As he wended his way from the laboratory detail to the cosmic generalization, Baldwin did not renounce his previous conclusions. He simply realized that they were inadequate to his task. He continually sought assurance that man and the universe were not random, amoral accidents,

---

[36] *American Neutrality*, pp. 24-28.

but had ordained and rational goals. Like Peirce, he could not get along without a teleological vision, and when he failed to find it on one level of investigation, he simply shifted to a higher plane, continually moving further from precise data toward larger and even more tenuous generalizations.[37]

As he cut himself off from particular scientific investigations, Baldwin also outgrew America. He taught at Princeton for ten years, from 1893 to 1903. He then took a chair at Johns Hopkins for five years but spent a good deal of his time travelling in Europe and Mexico. After he resigned the Hopkins chair, he spent his remaining years, to his death in 1935, in Europe. He was enraptured by tradition, pomp, and ceremony, and Europe possessed these whereas America could supply only industrial brashness and moral Puritanism. In Europe Baldwin found release from America's esthetic drabness, lack of individuality, and levelling mediocrity.[38]

To Baldwin's jealous American eyes, Oxford was the symbol of British excellence and tradition. One of the most memorable events of his life was the ceremony in which the University awarded him an honorary D.Sc. degree. Years later, in his autobiography, he was able to record every fascinating custom, every minute detail of dress and procedure of the convocation in the Sheldonian Theatre. So precious were his Oxford experiences that Baldwin made a chart of the twenty-three colleges where he had been asked to dine, showing their armorial designs and the names of the men who extended the invitations. The chart always hung on the wall above his desk.[39]

But it was France, not England, which most attracted Baldwin. His induction as one of the "immortals" of the Institute of France in 1910 surpassed even the Oxford ceremony in pomp and tradition. Baldwin spent the last twenty-five years of his life almost constantly in Paris, an untypical expatriate. He remained there throughout the war, trying to apologize for America's fail-

---

[37] Baldwin's development after the turn of the century into a metaphysician can be traced in *Development and Evolution* (1902), *Thought and Things* (1906-1911), and *Genetic Theory of Reality: Pancalism* (New York, 1914).
[38] For example, Baldwin's envious comment on Lord Balfour, *Between Two Wars*, I, p. 279.
[39] *Ibid.*, ch. 6.

ure to enter the struggle against Germany. After the war, he stayed in Paris to lecture at the Sorbonne and write his memoirs. Since the 1890s, Baldwin had been strongly influenced by French intellectuals—Ribot, Tarde, Gustave Le Bon, Lucien Levy-Bruhl, Pierre Janet, and later, Henri Bergson. What England was to most American intellectuals, and Germany to many others, France was to Baldwin, a source of both inspiration and confirmation for his own endeavors and ideas.[40]

In the French national character Baldwin found an almost perfect complement to the American. The French were much less cowed by the "social leviathan of convention" than either the Americans or the British. The French freedom from "collective moral sanctions" allowed individuality to come to full bloom in "sharpened theoretical insight, clarity and vigour of personal expression, and unequalled fertility of aesthetic invention." Greater freedom gave the French character a charm that the comparatively dull-witted, crudely utilitarian Americans lacked. "The entire French character," Baldwin enthusiastically believed, "is impregnated with this delicate essence of beauty." The difference between the two countries was the difference between "Rodin meditating before the *penseur*, and Bryan leading the Sunday-school singing class."[41]

The great shortcoming of the French was that their individuality, like the American emphasis on the collective, tended to extremes. French individualism, Baldwin complained, degenerated too often into social irresponsibility. French freedom allowed the "good man" to spurn the wrong, but this liberty was "dearly bought at the price of the weak man to whom this liberty offers a direful opportunity." Baldwin's ideal country was a kind of moral Atlantis, somewhere between French and American shores, where individuality and community were perfectly balanced. Whenever the Americans showed signs of a heightened individual creativity,

---

[40] *Between Two Wars,* I, ch. 10; *Social and Ethical Interpretations, passim,* but especially pp. 478, 505.

[41] Baldwin contrasts France and America in several pieces reprinted in *Between Two Wars,* II: "French and American Ideals," pp. 3-31; "Franco American Notes" (1918-1923), pp. 128-152. See also "An Aesthetic Contrast" (1916), *Ibid.,* pp. 90-92. *France and the War As Seen By An American* (New York, 1916).

Baldwin's sympathies drifted westward. Whenever the French seemed to lean toward "collectivism and deliberate eugenic purpose," the moral Atlantis moved closer to Europe. Baldwin took up residence in Paris, but his ideal country never existed. In 1923 he was still convinced that "We might profit by a dose of French *liberté*, with its apparent lack of restraint, and they by a dose of our 'liberty,' with its emphasis on public duty."[42]

The challenges to Baldwin's concept of community posed by France and America paled into insignificance in 1914. The difficulties he found with France and America could be corrected, but the Germans had so perverted social solidarity that they became the very personification of moral evil, the ultimate aberration of community, and the supreme threat to progress. Germany was a "beast, . . . prowling in the dark, to gore defenceless men." Baldwin spent the years between 1914 and 1917 assiduously propagandizing for American entry into the war and explaining American recalcitrance to the French. He worked for the French Ministry of Information, wrote public letters to Americans at home, and served as chairman of the Paris chapter of the American Navy League. The climax of his involvement came in 1916 when he and his family had to abandon the torpedoed *Sussex* in the English Channel.[43]

In Baldwin's eyes all the right was on the side of England and France. The Germans, he thought, were guilty of the most heinous crimes—murdering priests, poisoning wells, sending young girls into immoral slavery—these and "a hundred treacherous things." Baldwin claimed that he could not drink German beer or hear German music without experiencing nausea. For him, "the possibilities residing in the *Kultur*" were realized on Good Friday, 1918, when the Germans shelled the Paris church of St. Gervais, killing or maiming scores of worshippers.[44]

Germany, Baldwin bitterly claimed, completely corrupted social solidarity and community into a vicious statism and militar-

---

[42] "French and American Ideals," *Between Two Wars*, II, p. 12; "French Liberty and American," *Ibid.*, pp. 145-147.

[43] *Ibid.*, I, chs. 11-14; "The Voice of America" (1914), *Ibid.*, II, pp. 1-2; many of Baldwin's war writings are reprinted in *Ibid.*, II, pp. 32-128; see also *American Neutrality* and *France and the War*.

[44] *Between Two Wars*, I, pp. 185-188, II, pp. 42-43.

ism. German philosophy, he admitted, was quite correct in
making a distinction between values that were individual and
instrumental, on the one hand, and "over-individual" and eternal,
on the other. Without such a distinction, genuine social community was impossible, for there had to be a higher morality to bind
the members of a society together. The intellectual sin of the
Germans was to make the state the sole repository of over-individual and eternal values. The state, Baldwin claimed, was
merely the instrument of the society. It was not the nation, nor
could it ever claim to act exclusively for the nation. Government,
like other institutions, could not create community, but could
only help preserve already existing social harmony.[45]

The Germans erred and sinned doubly when they added a
Nietzschean ethic to their glorification of the state. This, Baldwin
claimed, put the German state "beyond good and evil," and made
the state's "will to power" the only test of the morality of its acts.
Baldwin was a theoretical nationalist. He realized that nations
and societies, in the Western world at least, were generally coter-
minus. But he believed that all nations, not any one, should be
self-determining and equal before international law. His hope
for peace was an international nationalism, a consort of nations
led by England, France and America, in which all would have
equal international rights and responsibilities. The Germans
threatened to make this impossible by diverting national sentiment from the broad channel of "generous social sympathy" into
the narrow and violent stream of national selfishness and aggression.[46]

Everywhere that Baldwin looked, he saw only excesses, both
of individualism and community—too much community in
America, too little in France, totally corrupt community in Germany. He elaborated, in theory, an incredibly delicate balance of
individual and society. In fact it was not a balance at all, but an
insistence on the virtues of both the individual and the community, without sacrifice on either side. Individualism meant genius

---

[45] *The Super State and the 'Eternal Values'* . . . *the Herbert Spencer Lecture
before the University of Oxford, 1916* (London, 1916).
[46] *Ibid.*; "Message from Americans Abroad to Americans at Home" (1916),
Between Two Wars, II, p. 83; *France and the War*, pp. 53-58.

and progress; society meant stability and harmony. Baldwin
wanted a civilization with all those antagonistic virtues. He asked
too much and was compelled to wander in search of a country
that fulfilled his theoretical demands. The war, then, was almost
a relief, for it enabled him to make an unalloyed commitment to
the allies, and relieved him, for a time of the disappointments of
his quest for the moral Atlantis.

Chapter 4

Edward Alsworth Ross: The Natural Man and the Community of Constraint

Edward Alsworth Ross was extraordinarily dolichocephalic. His head was 21.1 centimeters long, and only 15.2 centimeters broad, and he was proud that these measurements yielded a cephalic index of only 72, a figure that plainly set him off, in the parlance of his day, as a Nordic "type." The verdict of his head measurements was confirmed by his great height, six feet, four and one-half inches, and by his fair complexion. Only his dark eyes and hair, and the thinness of his nose suggested any racial "mixture," and these unpleasant suggestions could probably be accounted for by some "Alpine" ancestor. Ross was a midwesterner, born and raised among the "fiber of the people," clear-eyed folk with "home-bred notions of what is fit or decent or worthwhile." His family, he claimed, had been in America for two hundred years, and he could speak to Woodrow Wilson, without blushing, "as one of the Scotch-Irish strain to another of the Scotch-Irish strain." He was, proudly, a "one hundred per cent old-time American."[1]

When Ross examined America at the turn of the century, he professed surprise at finding his "stock," the "restless, striving,

---

[1] "Anthropomorphic Data," appended to Ross' autobiography, *Seventy Years of It* (New York, 1936), pp. 331-333; Ross, *Changing America* (New York, 1912), ch. 9; Ross to Woodrow Wilson, November 19, 1912, Ross papers, State Historical Society of Wisconsin, Madison (unless otherwise indicated, all citations of Ross manuscripts refer to this collection); Ross' patriotic description of himself is in the Madison *Capital Times*, April 18, 1935, and was reiterated by Ross in *Seventy Years of It*, p. 313.

doing Aryan," living in a social state. The ancestors of the "dolichocephalic blonds of the West" were fierce savages, unfettered
by social restraints. From among this "Germanic race" the most
unruly individualists had been, as Ross put it, "selected" by the
migration to Britain in which Teuton became Anglo-Saxon. Then,
in the second great migration to America, the most ruggedly individualistic Anglo-Saxons had been "selected." The American
frontier was yet another refining mechanism, which chose only
the hardiest, most self-reliant men for the trek to the west. Biologically, the northern European was an *"individualist . . .* in
blood and bone." The American, "product of the last, most
Westerly decanting of the Germanic race," was by inheritance
the world's purest individualist.[2]

Ross was deeply committed, emotionally and intellectually to
his idealized Aryan. And he was troubled, for the "blond beast"
appeared to be at bay. It was not natural, he thought, "for men
of the vigorous Northern breed to bend the neck" to social demands, and the fact that such men lived in society at all was
cause for amazement. The question of the age, for Ross, was
whether they could survive in an increasingly complex society of
great industries and burgeoning cities. The Anglo-Saxon in
America was being pressed on all sides, by yellow men from
Asia and by Slavs and Latins from Europe, men more adaptable
to the demands of life in factories and stock exchanges, New
Yorks and Chicagoes. Since the frontier was closed, there was no
escape room for a new "decanting" of the Anglo-Saxon. His survival now depended on his ability to succumb to discipline, to
round his jagged individualism to the specifications of a new age.

Ross wrote a program for survival, *Social Control: a Survey of
the Foundations of Order.* By the standards of the period, the
book was social "science," and it won him a very great reputation,
both among his sociological colleagues and a considerable public
audience. In fact, Ross had an even greater reputation in the
first decade of the twentieth century than Baldwin enjoyed in
the last decade of the nineteenth. But *Social Control* was more
than social science. It was a poorly disguised expression of Ross'

[2] Ross, *Social Control: a Survey of the Foundations of Order* (New York,
1901), pp. 3, 10, 17. Ross, like most of his contemporaries, used racial
jargon very loosely. Germanic race, Teuton, Aryan, Anglo-Saxon, and "old-
time American" were, for most purposes, practically interchangeable.

hopes and fears for the restless Aryan. More basically, and in more effective disguise, it was a piece of intellectual autobiography, an abstracted record of Ross' personal encounter with modern civilization. Ross was an Iowan, brought up in a small, isolated farming community among firm Presbyterians and other "old-time" Americans. In his mid-twenties he left Iowa, Presbyterianism, and America and confronted severe and unexpected challenges. He discovered speculative gloom in Arthur Schopenhauer and grim biological determinism in evolutionary science. Simultaneously, he met with factories and slums in Berlin, London, Baltimore, and Chicago. From a teacher in a tiny Iowa "collegiate institute," who had never seen a town larger than Cedar Rapids, Ross transformed himself in a few years into a famous intellectual, reasonably at home in the British Museum, a Berlin opera house, or before a Chicago audience. *Social Control* was, in part, his effort to explain to himself and to others just what happened to him, a record of his simultaneous encounter with a new learning and the industrial city.

In *Social Control* and its by-products, *The Foundations of Sociology* and *Social Psychology*, Ross bade a reluctant farewell to Iowa, to the unfettered dolichocephalic blond, and to Presbyterian precepts he had learned in his youth. He had found, painfully, that the simple manner of life, built on direct personal relations, which had worked successfully in Marion, Iowa, was hopelessly obsolete in urban and industrial society. He had also learned biological evolution and from it had extracted the equally painful lesson that man was not a moral agent with an innate conscience that fitted him for social life. The inescapable result of these twin lessons was that man's modern social state was unnatural and that society, to endure, must bend its members into new kinds of conformity, substituting its collective will for the private wills of its constituents.[3]

In a simple society (something like that of a German forest, or of Marion, Iowa), what Ross called "community" was as natural as the social life of a beehive. Men were bound together by ties of kinship and the intimacy of neighborhood. The city, and with it all modern life, replaced kinship and neighborhood with loose

---

[3] *The Foundations of Sociology* (New York, 1905); *Social Psychology: An Outline and Source Book* (New York, 1908).

"touch-and-go" relationships among men. The whole thrust of urban-industrial civilization was toward atomization, fracturing, and social strife. To avoid the "great crash" society must replace the "local solidarity" of village and parish with artificial social controls. In a natural community there were no conflicts between the individual and the group, and the individualistic Aryan could function fluently as a member. But in a society, as opposed to a community, order depended on constraint and the repression of the individual. Ross was nostalgic for the natural community and for the things it implied—the simplicities of Iowa and the virile freedom of the Aryan. His critique of individualism was reluctant and incomplete, but his conclusion was the same as Peirce's and Baldwin's—society must take precedence over the private individual.[4]

Ross was born December 12, 1866, in Virden, Illinois. His parents shifted about the middle west, treading the paths of dispersal and contraction so familiar in nineteenth-century America. His father took up a homestead in northeastern Kansas but quickly tired of sod-house farming, and the family returned to the Mississippi, to Davenport, Iowa. After a brief stay there, the Rosses moved to Marion, near Cedar Rapids. This unsettled pattern of life was irrevocably confirmed when Ross' parents both died, within two years of one another. At the age of eight, he was left an orphan—though not a destitute one, for he inherited the Kansas quarter-section and some other land in Illinois. He was handed about among various families in Marion until he finally landed in the home of M. D. Beach, an elderly justice of the peace. Squire Beach's younger wife, Mary, became the closest thing to a mother that Ross knew, and he was always (very self-consciously) a faithful correspondent of his "Dear Mamma."[5]

This potent lack of geographical and familial identity was redoubled by the fact that Ross was too bright and talented to be appreciated or even understood within the narrow cultural confines of Marion. He was a favorite among the girls in his rural school because he was free of the "coarse ways and speech" of

---

[4] *Social Control,* pp. 432-436.
[5] On Ross' early life see *Seventy Years of It,* ch. 1.

the other farm boys. The boys, he remembered in manhood, were jealous of his "better scholarship."[6] Indeed if Ross was any judge of his predicament, the entire community thought him somewhat peculiar. He never outgrew the resentful chip on his intellectual shoulder, the desire to show the folks back home. When he was experiencing his first professional success, he wrote to Mrs. Beach:

> I am anxious to convince the Walsers and Metcalfs and others of the old neighborhood back yonder that it pays to go in for something else than beer and coarse sports. Perhaps by this time they are beginning to think that "that little fool" was not quite so badly off in poring over books as they imagined.[7]

Ross was lucky enough to have the means to escape the constriction of Marion—his inheritance, carefully husbanded by an uncle. Drawing upon the sale of land, teaching school, and pitching hay in the summers, he made his way to a bachelor's degree at Coe College, a Presbyterian enterprise in Cedar Rapids. In the 1930s he looked back on Coe with disdain as a "tight little intellectual world . . . bounded by Presbyterianism, Republicanism, protectionism and capitalism." But this estimate was the product of fifty years of religious and political progressivism. In the 1880s the "tight little intellectual world" of Coe seemed expansively large; there were no "big boys" to scoff, no neighbors to cluck their tongues. And Ross thrived on his release. He was a member of a Greek-letter fraternity, president of the college band, and secretary of the literary society. He kept up a faithful church attendance and was earnestly active in prayer meetings during a college revival. Most important of all, the college took books and learning seriously and, within limits, without suspicion. There was, Ross exulted, even "a fine library, where any of the students may get a book between one and two o'clock every Friday afternoon."[8]

At Coe, Ross learned something of the world beyond Iowa, something no one in Marion had warned him of. Like Baldwin at Princeton, he was made aware that orthodox Presbyterian pre-

---

[6] *Seventy Years of It*, p. 5.
[7] Ross to Mrs. Beach, June 7, 1892.
[8] *Seventy Years of It*, ch. 2; Alexander Campbell, Ross' legal guardian, to Ross, September, 1882, and May 24, 1883; Ross to Mrs. Beach, January 15, 1882, October 14, 1883, March 2, 1884, December, 1885.

conceptions were being challenged by certain ill-defined notions, "Atheism, Agnosticism, etc." Ross was orthodox enough and surprised enough to be indignant. He made the unidentified atheists and agnostics—"scoffers," he called them—the victims of a denunciatory oration entitled "The New Foe of Thought." There had been, he claimed in good Protestant form, three centuries of steady progress in morals and science. But just when men were ready to pluck the finest fruits of this progress, the "scoffers" had arisen, threatening a "rapid breaking away from old beliefs and doctrines." In a passage so delightfully typical of the period that it might have been a parody, Ross stated the ethical dilemma of his age:

> We of today are sacrificing the products of the past with the same spirit in which the Huns or the Goth destroyed the monuments of beauty and art which adorned Imperial Rome. . . . They [the scoffers] would abolish the moral law implanted in man's conscience but would furnish no new code of rules for human guidance.[9]

In the spirit of his professors Ross was prepared in his college days to make a vigilant defense of "old beliefs and doctrines." But, like Baldwin and his other contemporaries, Ross soon learned his Darwinism and had to reconcile himself to the surrender of the "moral law implanted in man's conscience." The authority of conscience, indelibly imprinted on each man at birth, had been the ethical touchstone of the sanguine individualism of the first half of the nineteenth century. As Ross soon discovered, evolution stripped man of his innate conscience and left him ethically naked. The task of the intellectual might be difficult, but still was simple—to weave new ethical clothing to cover man's nakedness. As he matured, Ross saw the task as clearly as any one of his generation, and *Social Control* was his response.

At about the same time that he became aware of the intellectual challenge of the "scoffers," Ross learned that industrial capitalism was posing just as severe a threat to individualism. It is ironic that the things that concerned Ross most were those with which he had least direct contact as a college student. The atheists and agnostics whom he stigmatized in "The New Foe of Thought" were unidentified shadows, none of which lay across

---

[9] "The New Foe of Thought," an oration in Ross' college composition book, University Archives, Memorial Library, University of Wisconsin.

the fields of Iowa. And in another oration, "The Coming Slavery," Ross sounded the alarm against the dangers of massive industrial organizations, whose effects he had never encountered directly. From Herbert Spencer, Ross caught a glimpse of man enslaved by organization in the form of the modern state, and from Henry George he learned that Spencer was correct about the danger of enslavement, but wrong about its potential source. Ross concluded that the organizational threat came not from the political state but from within capitalism itself. The corporation, the capitalist with power over other men's lives, and the labor unions, these were the organizations that threatened man's individual freedom. The town of Pullman, Illinois, Ross claimed, was but an ominous foreshadowing of the future "slave utopia."[10]

The irony inherent in these college orations is double. It is ironic that Ross should have chosen as his subjects distant dangers that he had never confronted in concrete. But, in view of his later intellectual career, it is even more ironic that he should have taken such profoundly conservative positions. In time Ross learned that the "scoffers" were, in large measure, correct, and he contributed more than a little to undermining the individualistic morality of private conscience. He also learned in time that individualism in economics was dangerous and destructive and became a vocal sponsor of institutional restraints on the individual. His preoccupations remained the same—morality and organization. He abandoned, however, the stale defenses of individualism that he had made as a student and became, reluctantly, one of the limners of the new social man, member and product of his community.

In the meantime, however, Ross had to make a career for himself. He became a teacher and took a job at the Fort Dodge Collegiate Institute in Fort Dodge, Iowa. He gloated from the beginning of his stay that Fort Dodge "society" was "superior and select." He was always something of a snob, probably because of the uncertainties of his rather painful boyhood. He wrote home with pride of his contacts with the "society ladies" whom he taught history and German in his off hours. He joined the local Presbyterian church, taught Sunday school, and otherwise labored

---

[10] "The Coming Slavery," oration, in composition book, University of Wisconsin Archives.

to make himself a pillar of the town. He was very conscious of what he thought of as his "elevated" position, exulting that he was not a mere public school teacher. Everything was, he wrote home, "lovely, lovelier, loveliest."[11]

Ross taught an incredible variety of subjects—German, logic, history, American literature, arithmetic, physiology, mental philosophy (psychology), and natural philosophy (physics and general science). Still he had time to spare and bade fair to master a century's accumulation of science, philosophy, and literature in two short years. He began, properly for a young man in the 1880s, with Spencer's *First Principles* and went on "mastering Spencer's works." Then he went behind Spencer, directly to Darwin, whose *Descent of Man* made Ross a "thoroughgoing evolutionist." Intemperately, he read John William Draper's *Conflict of Science and Religion* and at the same time, Swedenborg. To further compound confusion between science and sensibility, he became an ardent disciple of Goethe and Carlyle. He was "enormously affected" by *The Sorrows of Young Werther*, and Carlyle seemed such a revelation that Ross prepared a paper on him for the local Chautauqua circle. The trauma Darwin might have caused was delayed, for the grim facts of evolution were clothed, first with the genial optimism of Darwin's own *Descent*, then with the broad assurances of Spencer, and, finally, with a romantic haze of Swedenborg, Goethe, and Carlyle.[12]

The reading was exciting. In fact, Ross's two years at Fort Dodge were intellectually the most fruitful of his life. Still there was a random and confused quality about it, and he began to look about for an intellectual base that might offer clarification and focus. For a talented young American in the 1880s, there was only one place to look, Germany, the "pinnacle of a good education." Even had there been no Germany to lure him away, Ross

---

[11] Ross to Mrs. Beach, November 2, 1886, December 12, 1886, February 22, 1888. When Ross joined the faculty, the college was changing from "a live exponent of practical Commercial Education" to a liberal arts college offering "thorough instruction by competent teachers in the classics, English, mathematics, German and sciences." Ross taught all these subjects from time to time.

[12] Ross to Mrs. Beach, September 21, 1886, October 3, 1886, January 1, 1887, February 6, 1887, March 8, 1887, May 8, 1887, January 22, 1888. Ross claimed that he read Carlyle's *French Revolution* six times; "passages of Sartor Resartus rang in my heart like cathedral bells."

probably would not have been able to sustain his life at Fort Dodge for very long. His days there were remarkably discontinuous. He could read Darwin in the afternoon and still be enthralled by a "great revival" in the evening. Or he might sorrow over young Werther in the morning and then go off to practice his part as a wax-figure villain for an "entertainment" by the ladies of the church. He was never unhappy at Fort Dodge, but he had no absorbing interest, nothing to give focus to his life. His teaching was quite mechanical, and there was no other outlet in Fort Dodge for his intellect. On one side of his life, there were his books and his intense excitement with the life of the mind. On the other side, there were only the meager offerings of Fort Dodge. Germany was, at bottom, a hope that his inner life and his outer circumstances could be integrated.[13]

In the fall of 1888 Ross sold his Kansas quarter-section for about $1800 and set out for Berlin. He wasted no time in New York but made his way as directly as possible to Berlin, where he spent almost all of his German year. The city was a revelation. He felt that he had cut through a veil and could now touch modern life at its vital center. Marion, Coe College, Fort Dodge, all his previous experience, had been, he realized, a mere incomplete preparation for life. On New Year's Eve, 1888, he joined swirling crowds of Berliners to drink and shout in the new year. It was a memorable night. "I saw and learned as much about life in the great cities as I had learned altogether before. . . . It beat anything I ever saw." After Berlin, he concluded, a small town in America would be unbearable. The "petty world of reality" of Marion or Fort Dodge would utterly stifle all desire to study or think. Berlin, by contrast, was a glittering summation of all the careers that might lie at the end of the paths of thought:

> The long lines of brilliant electric light globes, the rows of brilliant shop windows, the omnibusses, the carriages, the streams of pedestrians —all this made me exult. "Hurrah!" I cried to myself, "This is what you are preparing for. You will be one of similar streams of humanity in the cities of the Great Republic. You shall be in the tide. Work and wait and watch."[14]

---

[13] Ross to Mrs. Beach, November 25, 1886, February 20, 1887, March 8, 1887, November 24, 1887.

[14] Durland and King, attorneys, Centralia, Kansas, to Ross, September 1, 1888; Ross to Mrs. Beach, January 10, 1889; German diary, January 26, 1889.

But Berlin was not all glitter and promise. It was something new, a surprise and a shock. Ross' frontal encounter with the great city left marks on his consciousness that shaped his entire career. In Berlin he experienced, for the first time, loneliness, a complete lack of personal ties—even ties of jealousy or contempt—which had characterized Iowa. "The two most awful desolations in the world," he confided to his diary, "are the desert and the great city." Added to the loneliness, intensifying it, was the sheer multivariety of Berlin, the unaccustomed and shocking contrasts between wealth and poverty, style and crudity, cleanliness and filth. "The luxury of the city does not offset its misery. The theater does not compensate for the bagnio. The philharmonic does not balance the dive, the palace does not compensate for the tenement, the electric light does not replace the sun." Berlin suffered from these faults no more than an American city might, but Berlin labored under the additional disability of being European. Like all the rest of the Continent, Berlin was cankered over by the past, tight in the grip of "absurd and antiquated custom." "Oh, what rot!" Ross exclaimed to his diary when Berlin went into public mourning for the crown prince of Austria. "I am stuck on America," he admitted, for America was fresh and alive, and Europe was decadent and gloomy.

> I feel I must get out of this despair laden atmosphere very soon. Poor Europe is a charnal-house, with an air that is heavy with decay and death. My heart keeps crying "Back to America, the land of hope, of optimism, of progress, of nature, of freedom, of will, and of wealth! Back to the beautiful bubble! Back to the people still left in the sweet illusion of hope! Home or die!"[15]

Ross' anxious longing for America was the product of severe intellectual shock. He had gone to Europe full of hope. In his Fort Dodge reading what he called his "rank corn and cotton optimism" had been confirmed in one way or another, by Spencer and Darwin, Goethe and Carlyle. In Germany he expected to find hope still more firmly and systematically confirmed. Hegel was the logical place to begin, for Hegel offered affirmations even more strident than Spencer's. Had Ross been able to understand and love Hegel after the fashion of William T. Harris or Josiah Royce, his intellectual career would have taken a markedly different shape. But he

15 Ross to Mrs. Beach, January 10, 1889; German diary, December, 1888, and December 7, 1888, February 1, 1889, May 9, 1889.

found Hegel "pure nonsense" from the very beginning, and left off trying to fathom it precisely on page 185 of the *Phenomenology*.[16]

Ross' defection from the study of Hegel meant more than the simple abandonment of one philosophical point of view. His closing the covers of the *Phenomenology* led eventually to the rejection of speculative philosophy altogether. Ross turned directly from Hegel to Eduard von Hartmann and Arthur Schopenhauer. Von Hartmann was especially distressing. His principal claim was that individual consciousness and identity were purely the products of pain. Life, in von Hartmann's view, was a vast web of vanity and deceit, and the most vain, deceitful enterprise of all was conscious ratiocination. Man's only valid option was to abandon altogether his conscious efforts to be happy and especially to abandon any attempt to make sense of the world.[17]

Even alone, Schopenhauer and von Hartmann were a "great motive to despair," but the truly devastating thing about their pessimism was its profound implications for evolutionary science. Before he went to Germany, Ross had read the evolutionary tale through a protective screen of gentle, optimistic speculation. He went to Berlin prepared to find, in Hegel or elsewhere, an even more pleasing mantle with which to cover what Darwin called the "tangled bank." What he encountered, instead, was a ruthless command to strip the natural world of all speculative apologies. The emergent picture was grim: "It is plain that the swift spread of science has brought men into a new universe. Few there are that can adorn the new home with remnants saved from the old. For most men, the universe which science tells of rises about them unsightly and barn-like, with bare walls and naked rafters."

Ross, in his Berlin days at least, was intellectually courageous, even reckless. He read clearly the ultimate message of evolution. The brutal, inescapable facts of biology spelled quick death to the notion of an inviolable individual soul. And, with the ideal of the individual soul, the illusion of individual freedom must also die. "Science," Ross said in perhaps the best lines he ever wrote,

> finds the soul not a spiritual unit, but a treacherous compound of strange contradictions and warring tendencies, with traces of spent passion and vestiges of ancient sins, with echoes of forgotten deeds and survivals

16 Ross to Mrs. Beach, January 10, 1889; *Seventy Years of It*, ch. 4.
17 German diary, December 20, 1888; Ross, "Turning Towards Nirvana: The Pessimistic Attitude in Europe," *Arena*, 4 (November, 1891), p. 740.

of vanished habits. We are possessed not by demons but by the dead.
. . . We are followed by the shades of our ancestors who visit us, not
with midnight squeak and gibber, but in broad noonday, speaking with
our speech, and doing with our deed. We are bound to a destiny fixed
before birth, and choice is the greatest of all illusions.[18]

Thus "home or die!" was more than an empty slogan for Ross.
America, that "beautiful bubble," was still in the rapturous clasp
of the "sweet illusion of hope." And it was to illusion that Ross
committed himself. Von Hartmann or Schopenhauer might be
correct, the world might be a monstrous deceit, but what could
a man gain from mourning and crying vanity? It would be far
better, Ross decided, to forego reasoning altogether than to be
emasculated by it. If the conclusions of reflective inquiry were
completely debilitating, then "thinking is an evil of a very positive
kind. Consciousness—the consciousness of strict reason—is a disease. . . . The texture of a happy life is woven of dreams, of instincts unrepressed, of passions yielded to, of abandonment to
the moment, whims, caprices, a vivid sense of freedom, foolish
and self-willed acts." Frustrated in his quest for a sensible metaphysics, unable to accept the stark, deterministic universe of
evolutionary science, Ross committed himself to a philosophy of
the irrational, a celebration of the act. He might, he acknowledged,
have reflective moments when he saw through the "deceit of life."
But when he entered life, he would leave off reflection and
"utterly give myself up to the great human feelings."[19]

Armed with such views, Ross might have imported into America a personal *fin de siecle*. But his Iowa good sense exerted its
hold. "Instincts unrepressed" and "passions yielded to" turned
out to mean nothing more outlandish than a possibility that he
might run for Congress. His celebration of the capricious act was
translated into a determination to do something about concrete
problems—"the problems of labor, government, food, fuel, immigration, church, education, technique, art, literature, morals."
Ross committed himself to a career of political social reform:

---

[18] Ranulph Marrett, an English student and anthropologist with whom Ross
struck up an acquaintance in Berlin, to Ross, June 26, 1889; "Turning Toward Nirvana," p. 739.
[19] German diary, December 20, 1888, April 10, 1889, July 5, 1889.

The philosopher dying of loneliness and purposelessness . . . envies the heat of passion, intensity of desire, energy of will, warmth of love and fierceness of hate felt by those struggling and shouting amid the multitude.

He rejected, by an act of will and not of reason, the speculative gloom of Europe's decline. He grasped the hope of America and the future—knowing, all the while, that the hope was an illusion and America a "beautiful bubble." He had tasted the bitter fruit of knowledge. Now he would recover innocence in action.[20]

The immediate result of his decision was calm. Once he had committed himself to an active life of social service, Ross could relax and enjoy Europe. "Now that I have decided to rush into the fray and live in the thickest of the battle of life, instead of in academic halls, I can enjoy the short respite of study and contemplation without being tormented by my former doubts . . . Wonderful, wonderful days!" Opera, music, the theater, the university, reading were no longer wasteful excursions into idleness or threats to peace of mind. "Oh! What glorious romantic days and nights these are! would that they might last forever." His conscience was clear. He had promised himself a useful, active, and American life. Now he could give in completely to the tempting luxury of Europe: "Here I could be content to eat lotus."[21]

After the close of the university year, Ross set out on the customary walking tour through Switzerland and Italy. This completed, he spent a month in Paris, another in London, and by December, 1889 he was back in the United States in time to spend Christmas with a Coe classmate, J. E. Barber, preparing for the ministry at Andover Theological Seminary. Barber somehow changed the whole course of Ross' life. Ross had vowed to forsake the sterile academic life and to "rush into the fray." Specifically, he planned to study law and then go into politics, but Barber convinced him that at Johns Hopkins the academic study of social problems was exhibiting an unaccustomed and virile urgency in the person of the economist Richard T. Ely. Barber prevailed on Ross to go to Baltimore and join Ely's "seminary."[22]

---

[20] Ross to Mrs. Beach, January 10, 1889; German diary, December 10, 1888, January 19, 1889, July 5, 1889.

[21] German diary, May 15, 1889, July 9, 1889.

[22] *Seventy Years of It*, pp. 39-40.

Ely was stimulating, encouraging and, most important, deeply committed to social reform. Johns Hopkins, Ross found, suffered from neither the pettiness of Fort Dodge nor the purposeless gloom of Berlin. He prepared a dissertation on public finance and accepted a teaching job at Indiana University. A year and a half after he returned from Berlin intent on politics, Ross was permanently drawn into a university career. He taught at Indiana for one year, at Cornell for another, and then in 1893 received a call from David Starr Jordan at Stanford. The invitation to Stanford was an academic plum, and Ross' stature was even further enhanced by the publication of his dissertation on *Sinking Funds* by the American Economic Association. During his brief stay at Cornell, he was elected secretary of the Association, to succeed Ely. At twenty-three, Ross had vowed to quit academic life; at twenty-seven he was a Ph.D., an experienced university teacher with the beginnings of a professional reputation.[23]

He was not disturbed by this reversal, however, because he was able to shape his vocation to satisfy his Berlin resolves. He used his professorships as bases from which he could conduct frequent sorties into public life. Armed with his developing reputation and the credentials of a scientist, he constantly ventured off the campus to make aggressive pronouncements on social problems. At Indiana, he gave a series of lectures in Indianapolis, defending "the interests of the common people and especially the farmers." While at Cornell, he published a call to action, "The Reform Spirit," in the student magazine, and he lectured to Rochester audiences on labor, socialism, tax and monetary reform, and municipal reform. On leave from Stanford during the summer of 1896, he wrote a pamphlet supporting silver coinage, and 60,000 copies were printed by the Democratic central committee and distributed as campaign literature. In California Ross spoke to citrus farmers and San Francisco workingmen on free silver and municipal ownership of public utilities. For him the university was a reforming institution and the professor a reformer.[24]

---

[23] *Seventy Years of It*, ch. 5; Ross to Mrs. Beach, April 13, 1890, November 26, 1891, May 14, 1892, June 7, 1892, October 17, 1896.
[24] *Seventy Years of It*, Chs. 5, 6; Ross to Mrs. Beach, November 26, 1891, May 4, 1892, June 7, 1892, October 17, 1896; W. H. Alvord, chairman California Democratic State Central Committee, to Ross, November 2, 1896; circular from Democratic Press Bureau, September 25, 1896, endorsing Ross' silver pamphlet, *Honest Dollars* (Chicago, 1896).

In fact reform was more important to Ross than academic economics. He grew restless and dreamed of earning a living by writing on social issues. Economics, he lamented, omitted "human values," and after 1892 his interest in the subject waned. He introduced sociology courses at Stanford, and in 1896 the title of his chair was formally changed from economics to social science.[25]

Lester Frank Ward exerted a crucial influence over Ross' change of discipline. Ross had first read Ward's massive *Dynamic Sociology* while he was a student at Johns Hopkins. The intellectual relationship established by his profound response to *Dynamic Sociology* assumed a more personal and concrete quality when he married Ward's niece. Ross and Ward corresponded heavily during the most crucial years of Ross' life, the 1890s, when Ross was doing the intellectual spade-work for his most important books.

Ward's *Dynamic Sociology* and *Psychic Factors of Civilization* affected Ross deeply, largely because they went to the root of his Berlin disillusionment. Ward comprehended ·the reason for the stress of Berlin—no adequate rationale could be found in the nature of things for human civilization. Neither philosophical nor biological speculation could discover any sufficient grounds for social values. But instead of surrendering to these frightening discoveries, Ward opted, as Ross had instinctively done, for action. Society, Ward taught, is artificial, not "real" in any metaphysical or even biological sense. But in the very artificiality of society lay the opportunity for action. Society, if artificial, was subject to control. It could be altered by the exertion of the will.

Ross had reached the same conclusion in Berlin, but by mental fiat; Ward offered extensive and technical premises. For both men, but especially for Ross, sociology was preeminently a guide to action, not a disinterested inquiry, a program and not a discipline. When he changed his academic title from economics to sociology, Ross did so in commitment to "the deadly enmity of sociology to the laissez-faire, 'natural rights,' 'freedom of contract' philosophy which is one of the bulwarks of vested interests." Sociology was as much a social and political movement as socialism—"The socialists are too extreme. . . . The sociologists will pass them on the home stretch." Ross shared the belief of many

---

[25] *Seventy Years of It,* pp. 50, 56, 81.

of the social thinkers of the period (men like Ely, John R. Commons, Albion Small, Dewey, Roscoe Pound, and Thorstein Veblen) that he could be objective and still passionate, scientist and still progressive, that social science could be both data and program, law and plan of action. This faith was the intellectual context within which Ross worked.[26]

Just before Christmas, 1894 Ross sat in an alcove of the Stanford Library and jotted down a list of the thirty-three different ways he thought societies controlled their individual members. For the next six years, he lived his intellectual life within the confines of this list. He published twenty-seven articles on social control in the *American Journal of Sociology* and more in other periodicals. He pruned the list until he had reduced it to more manageable proportions, and by 1899 the basic structure of *Social Control* was complete. Ross then spent a year in Paris and London, gathering more exotic data to support his conclusions. By November, 1900 he was finished. With Ely's conscientious help, he found a publisher for the all-too-lengthy manuscript and so launched his career as a major American thinker.[27]

The fact that Ross began with a list of thirty-three items revealed one of his most distinctive qualities of mind. His violent reaction in Germany against speculative philosophy had been a vivid exemplification of the same mental set, the same tendency to think in particulars, or at best in lists of particulars, to describe instance at the expense of theory. Peirce's social ideals were set within an elaborate epistemological and metaphysical realism and a full-blown system of ethics and logic. In Baldwin's work social ideas hinged on the mechanics of the "dialectic of personal growth," and society was systematically related to biological, even universal evolution. Ross, by contrast, worked with what he thought were the simple facts. His technique was descriptive, and his data were historical and anthropological, not biological or

---

[26] Ross to Ward, December 11, 1895, May 30, 1905, September 16, 1905.
[27] Ross to [?] Kawabe, a Japanese scholar interested in translating *Social Control*, January 12, 1915; Ross to Ely, February 2, 1900, August 6, 1900; *Seventy Years of It*, pp. 56-58.

metaphysical. Social phenomena were to him *sui generis,* not extensions of observations of protozoa or of a theory of reality.

The most striking result of Ross' ruthlessly nominalist method was a certain rugged voluntarism. Peirce and Baldwin built into their social theories virtual guarantees of progress. For Peirce, the self-correcting method of science assured the eventual triumph of truth and community, if only inquiry endured. Baldwin's dialectics favored the emergence of higher and higher "ideal selves" living in progressively better societies. Ross shared none of this optimism. Society, he thought, was a fabric, not a growth, a fabric woven by the wilfull, precarious efforts of men. Men might fail or be crushed by natural disaster, and their societies might be rent into meaningless thread and lint. Or they might simply err and create societies that were stagnant or regressive. Ross clearly identified himself with a new style in American thought. He believed, with men like Herbert Croly and Walter Lippmann, that the natural condition of things was chaotic drift, without direction and especially without any built-in assurances of progress. The condition of drift could be corrected, as Lippmann put it, only by willing mastery.[28]

This is not to say, of course, that Peirce and Baldwin were the naive victims of an American "innocence," of which Ross was able to disabuse himself. Their optimism was of a cosmic variety, and they could be thoroughly pessimistic about the short run. In fact Ross was more nearly satisfied with turn-of-the-century America than either Peirce or Baldwin. Peirce was a disenchanted critic, whereas Ross was a committed reformer. Baldwin went so far as to expatriate himself, whereas time and travel only made Ross more "stuck on America." Ross' hopeful commitment to reform was the product of his lack of assurance. America in 1901 meant more to him than to Peirce or Baldwin, simply because he lacked Peirce's faith in the infinitely long run or Baldwin's vision of an eventual moral Atlantis. His world, therefore, was one of continuous crisis, of fear that the last chance might be lost on any single drawing of a card. "*Society,*" he thought, "*is always in the presence of the enemy.*"[29]

---

[28] *Social Control,* pp. 60, 432-436; *Foundations of Sociology,* pp. 42-47, 102; cf. Croly, *Promise of American Life* (New York, 1909), especially pp. 21-22; Lippmann, *Drift and Mastery* (New York, 1914).
[29] The italics are Ross'. *Social Control,* 190.

What he was groping toward, without a clear view of the result, was a complete rejection of the teleological and evolutionary matrices that had encased Western social thought for centuries. He gave up the idea of an inevitable progress, an "ameliorative drift," built into society either by a creator's final cause or by the evolutionary survival of higher forms. Ross was an instinctive progressive in politics, but progress for him was something wrung out of a reluctant universe. The various "optimistic accounts of sociality," he thought, were fatally naive. Their faith in progress rested on the badly mistaken presumption that man was, by nature, a fit subject for social life and, hence, for social improvement.[30]

In the eighteenth century, as Ross viewed it, this presumption had been based on the idea that men had an innate sense of right and wrong, a "set of commandments etched on the soul." The discovery of other cultures with varying standards of morality had dealt a stunning blow to such a simple account. Moralists had then tried to fill the resultant vacuum, especially after Kant, with the assertion that the "soul" was at least endowed with a generalized "sense of *oughtness*," a conscience. But Darwin had demonstrated the emptiness of the idea of conscience, and the search had then begun for a theory of man's morality and fitness for society that would take instinct and emotion fully into account.

In the decades after the *Origin of Species* the most popular solution had been to posit a social instinct, such as "consciousness of kind" or "instinctive sympathy," as part of the biological endowment of each new man. Spencer had written the most complete brief for evolutionary man as a sociable and progressive animal. Man's instincts, according to Spencer, were both egoistic and altruistic. The mechanics of survival were gradually breeding the egoism out, and men would eventually live together in harmony, because each constituent unit of society would be perfectly fit for a common life. In time, Ross thought, social philosophers would realize that defining the human personality as a mixture of egoism and altruism was as vacuous as defining milk as curds and whey. Then a new naturalistic rationale for

---

[30] "Ameliorative drift" was, of course, a slap at Spencer, but it would fit as well any social thinker who presumed a built-in, directional progress. *Social Control*, p. 60; *Foundations of Sociology*, pp. 102, 257.

society would be sought. Already, from various sides had come new and "charming tales of the mutual aid of ants, beavers, and prairie dogs," suggesting the presence of specifically social instincts in man.[31]

Ross set himself against any variety of naturalism. He acknowledged that in the most primitive societies there existed a kind of natural order, founded on instinctive sympathy or gregariousness. But natural order was hopelessly obsolete in civilization. In urban life, especially, "social order finally parts company with the sociable impulse." The social order of civilized men flowed from no natural spring. It was something society imposed on its individual members and was thoroughly unnatural. "In a certain way," Ross wrote to Ward, "I have had to fight over again the kind of battle you had to fight, viz., the essential artificiality of civilization. You proved it for civilization in general. I seek to prove it for moral civilization."[32]

Man was born and lived out his life within the artificial frame of society. In fact even the human self was a social product. Ross knew little of the psychology of the self being developed by Peirce, Baldwin, James, Dewey, and others. But he did know its conclusion—the self was not an original entity, but the product of social experience. Self-consciousness, personality, even the most rudimentary capacity for thought and emotion, Ross thought, could not arise outside society. "Romancers," he recalled, had often speculated on the way a child would mature if it were cut off from all common life. Ross accepted the answer of what he called the "newer psychology." The "psychic development of the child would be arrested at a stage not far above idiocy." To be human, in any recognizable sense, a man must first be social.[33]

Ross used Baldwin's concept of the socially developed self. It was convenient, and it saved him the difficult work of con-

---

[31] *Social Control,* 5; *Foundations of Sociology,* pp. 260-271.
[32] Ross to Ward, December 11, 1895, *American Sociological Review,* 3 (June, 1938), p. 391; *Social Control,* p. 19.
[33] *Social Control,* pp. 23, 64, 315-324; *Foundations of Sociology,* p. 256; *Social Psychology,* p. 11. Ross was not competent in experimental or clinical psychology, and he did not follow the new developments in technical detail. In fact the only formal structure of *Social Control* was provided by the already outmoded "faculty psychology" which Ross had learned from the textbooks of McCosh and Noah Porter. He divided the means of social control into those that worked on the will, the judgment (intellect), and the feelings.

structing his own theory of self-consciousness. But there was a fundamental distinction between the two men. Baldwin believed that the dialectic of personal growth penetrated to the most distant corners of mind and emotion, making man a thoroughly social being. Ross, wary of such an optimistic analysis, thought that the social self was a mere veneer.

> There is an unreclaimed jungle in man, from which wild impulses break forth and lay waste the well trimmed fields. Despite the well-trimmed, prepossessing lawns in front, there are unpleasant, slimy things lurking in the rear fens and undergrowth of the human soul.

The individual's social self was just as artificial as the society which created it, and society to preserve itself must continually "fight the devil with fire." *Social Control* was an inventory of the various forms of fire at the disposal of society.[34]

Some of the means of social control that Ross examined were based on constraint and punishment. Most prominent in this category was the law, the overt frame of control in almost every society. In the interstices of the law there was custom, carrying almost as much compulsive force as law. And, since there were always a few individuals who sinned against society and evaded detection in their own lifetimes, almost all societies had a set of formal religious beliefs which guaranteed eventual justice in rewards and punishments. Ross freely acknowledged the necessity of such constraints, but progress meant to him a gradual replacement of overt threat and force by more subtle techniques of social control. Law, custom, and institutional religion had the major disadvantage of emphasizing the latent antagonism of individual and community. Ross preferred means of control that gently persuaded the individual to give up his own ends in favor of the necessities of the community.[35]

There were, he thought, several such mechanisms—public opinion, education, the creation of ideals of behavior by art, by the example of extraordinary individuals, and even by the old

---

[34] *Social Control,* pp. 23-25, 197. Ross' debt to Baldwin was parallelled by a similar debt to Baldwin's master, Tarde. In 1901 Ross was contemplating a book on social psychology, but he was reluctant to write it because it would be "half founded on him." Ross to Ward, July 7, 1901, *American Sociological Review,* 11 (December, 1946), p. 747. Ross resolved this problem by writing a *Social Psychology* which contained almost no psychology.
[35] *Social Control,* chs. 11, 12, 15.

friend of his Berlin days, illusion. Often, a frank process of "enlightenment" could replace the constraints of law. Man could be convinced that his own self-interest and the interests of the community coincided, that what appeared to be a private gain at society's expense would turn out, eventually, to be both a private and a social loss. "Often," Ross believed, "a man misbehaves from mere shortsightedness, and if we can get the myope to consider his welfare *in the long run*, he will become a well conducted member of the community."[36]

But Ross reserved his most passionate encomium for the form of social control he called "social religion"—as against institutional religion, that "paid ally of the policeman." The message of social religion was the essential and ideal unity of all men in a common life, the brotherhood of men under the fatherhood of God. As Ross put it,

> Only in social life does man realize his true and complete self. Hence, to seek the Kingdom of God and his righteousness, i.e., to realize perfect harmony with one's brethren, is the first concern of the disciple.

This was the "social affirmation of Jesus," the best and purest doctrine of all the "higher religions," and especially of Christianity. It was the "sacred flame of love," kept barely alive in the church until the middle of the nineteenth century when it had at last caught in full brilliance. Social religion was a demanding mental and emotional discipline, and Ross thought it could thoroughly regenerate only an elite fraction of society. But such an elite, charged with such a faith, might set the ideals for others, and Jesus' social contribution might become a way of life for society.[37]

---

[36] *Social Control*, p. 291, chs. 10, 16, 20, 22-27.

[37] *Ibid.*, ch. 16, especially pp. 204, 206. Ross conceived his mission as something like that of a minister preaching the progressive social gospel. "Most of all," he wrote to Ely of *Social Control*, "preachers will get the book. It throws floods of light on what they are dealing with, viz., the regeneration of men." Ross made similar remarks on the closeness of sociology and the social gospel in public addresses. "The Improvement of Theological Education," draft of a speech, ca. November 2, 1912, in the Ross papers. Ross' concept of the "social affirmation of Jesus" was lifted almost bodily from one of the leading publicists of the social gospel, Shailer Mathews. Mathews' *The Social Teachings of Jesus: an Essay in Christian Sociology* (New York, 1897), was published serially in the *American Journal of Sociology* just as Ross set to work on *Social Control*.

The compelling advantage of the methods of enlightenment and
social religion was that they did not destroy individual freedom
but elevated it. They could cross what Ross thought was the
"asses' bridge" of social philosophy, the bridge between private
and social ends. The gently persuasive means of control might
end the quarrel between the individual and the community by
bringing the two into a harmony of ideals and interests. Such an
eventuality was Ross' fondest hope. Every instinct he had rebelled
at the fetters he was helping to place on the individual. His mind
was tightly drawn between his affection for the individual, the
free Aryan, and Iowa, at one pole, and, at the other, his recognition of the necessities of Darwinism and the city.

Social Control was written to forge "coil upon coil to entangle
the unruly one," a scientific guide to "man-quellers." But playing
beneath the surface of the book was a keen apprehension of the
debilitating effects of control on the individual. The art of domes-
ticating the human animal might suceed only too well, and man
might lose his original vigor and strength. There might, Ross
feared, be a mental and moral parallel to the physical "shrivelling
of the female breast with the advent of the patent baby food, the
decay of the teeth with the perfecting of dentistry, the degen-
eration of the eye with the improvement of spectacles." Ross
identified the individual with nature, and he was an outdoorsman
with a love for wild nature that children of the city like Peirce
and Baldwin never felt. Social control was a necessity, but as it
successfully hedged the individual about with artificial braces, it
would favor the "weak spine" and soften the "fiber of character."
The blond beast, the self-confident Iowan, might succumb finally
to "southern" evils, forsaking the hardy virtue of hearth, field, and
forest for the giddiness of the plaza, the foyer, and the street.[38]

Ross would have preferred to cast his lot with the free and
self-sufficient individual. In fact he consoled himself with the
thought that he was only helping build a "genuine individuality"

---

[38] *Social Control,* pp. 304, 437-440; *Foundations of Sociology,* pp. 106-109;
Social Psychology, pp. 58, 87-88. Ross' remark on the female breast has a
bitter autobiographical significance. His first child died in 1897 because,
he claimed, his wife's breast milk was insufficient and no satisfactory "patent"
food could be found for the child. Ross to Mrs. Beach, April 2, 1896,
November 28, 1897.

by making men aware of their social origins and obligations. Only irresistible pressures forced him into the quest for community, and *Social Control* was a painful book for him to have to write. Fear was played off against fear, fear of both individual and society. Personal inclinations pushed Ross one way, toward the individual, but history and circumstance forced him another, toward a reluctant submission to the demands of community.

Social Control, more than Peirce's essays or Baldwin's books on social psychology, was a response to the American situation. The American character, Ross believed, had been tempered by the "pitiless sifting" of conquering the west. But the west was now closed, the free land gone, and the seductive vices of a settled and urban life threatened to reduce America to the decadence that Ross had encountered in Berlin. Already, the coastal areas were morally soft. Only the midwest retained the strength bred into it by the American experience, and its brightest and healthiest youth was being lured into the numerous waiting Sodoms and Gomorrahs.[39]

In these cities and in the nation of cities, the "folk-mass" became a "dangerous compound ready to explode at a touch." Anglo-Saxon, rural America was endowed with a precious homogeneity. But the new America was being overrun by immigrants from southern and eastern Europe, Catholic in religion, living in industrial slums, threatening to eat away the old fund of common ancestry, common faith, and common experience which made Iowa so stable. The new society was volatile, given to fads and crazes at best and, at worst, threatening mob violence and a fiery struggle among its unassimilated elements.

> The antipathies of sects threaten to tear society to pieces. The drawing apart into opposing camps of poor and rich, capitalist and worker, functionary and citizen, civilian and soldier, as well as the race enmity of white and black, or yellow and white, or Christian and Jew, summons society to act or perish.[40]

---

[39] The frontier, or, more accurately, the closing of the frontier, was a prominent theme of *Social Control*. In 1900 Ross did not know directly of Frederick Jackson Turner, though by 1902 he had read Turner's 1893 essay, "The Significance of the Frontier in American History." On the frontier, see *Social Control*, pp. 17, 42, 83-84, 86-87; *Foundations of Sociology*, pp. 325, 386, 395; *Social Psychology*, pp. 213-214; *Sin and Society* (New York, 1907). p. 132; *Changing America*, p. 5.

[40] *Social Control*, pp. 51-56, 393-394; *Foundations of Sociology*, p. 106; *Changing America*, pp. 96-97.

Ross answered the summons in *Social Control,* but he did so reluctantly. It was not a great book, but it was a promising one, and another man might have used it as an entering wedge for more research and better books on the conflict of society and the individual. But the effort cost Ross too dearly. He still had enough momentum to complete *Foundations of Sociology* and *Social Psychology,* but his career peaked at the turn of the century in his first real book. When it had won him academic preferment and a certain amount of public acclaim and personal security, he frittered away the rest of his long life on muckraking, textbooks, and travel books. Ross paid a tribute to intellectual necessity with *Social Control.* The payment freed him for a more exciting, less intellectually demanding. commerce with "issues"—progressive politics and trusts, immigration and "race suicide," the different kinds of social revolutions in China, Latin America, and Mexico.

Ross' life after 1900 takes on an almost satirically ironic cast when it is set against *Social Control.* The book was written in response to historical necessities that seemed, in the 1890s, irresistible. After it was completed, however, Ross spent most of his time trying to evade or even reverse the history that had made it necessary. His travels, for example, were obvious exercises in evasion. His trip to Europe in 1899 (this time in the company of a stabilizing wife) convinced him once and for all that Europe was hopelessly decadent and, worse, might well be a preview of what America was to become now that the frontier was lost. So Ross spent the rest of his life carefully avoiding Europe. He was one of the most travelled men of his time, but he sought out the peripheries of civilization rather than touch its corrupt heart again. China in 1910, South America in 1913-1914, Russia in 1917, Mexico in 1922, Africa in 1923-1924, around the world on a shipboard "floating university" in 1928-1929, Tahiti in 1932—anywhere but old Europe. And wherever in his travels Ross encountered concrete examples of firm community control of the individual—whether "familism" in China or collective farming in Russia—he was appalled and longed for the American midwest.[41]

---

[41] Ross to Mrs. Beach, October 15, 1898. Ross' travel books were *The Changing Chinese: the Conflict of Oriental and Western Culture in China* (New York, 1915); *South of Panama* (New York, 1915); *Russia in Upheaval* (New York, 1918); *The Russian Bolshevik Revolution* (New York, 1921); *The Russian Soviet Republic* (New York, 1923). On "familism," see *Changing*

Ross tried other ways to stave off history. The threat of violent class struggle was one of the most potent of the social facts that had necessitated *Social Control*. If the threat could be obviated, then the individual might enjoy more freedom from social demands. Ross had the additional motive of having been forced out of Stanford in 1901 by the "vested interests," in one of the most spectacular academic firings in American history. So, at the University of Wisconsin, he became a muckraker, assailing the abuses of industrial capitalism, demanding more government control of corporations so that the individual might be more free. Looking back from the 1930s, Ross proudly claimed that he, thirty-three other men, and Ida Tarbell had "saved the day." They had publicized the evils of industrial capitalism, fostered reforms, and so had avoided a "huge, futile social blow-up in our country, followed by iron military repression." Ross had traversed a tortuous circle back to the cry of alarm against industrialism he had raised in his college oration on "The Coming Slavery." Once more, he was defending the individual against society.[42]

Ross also fell in ardently behind Theodore Roosevelt, because Roosevelt seemed to be the only statesman who could fend off class struggle. There were other reasons. Roosevelt paid attention to intellectuals: Ross' invitation to Oyster Bay came late in 1914. Like Ross, Roosevelt loved the west and old America and was publicly worried about "race suicide," a phrase Ross claimed to have invented. Roosevelt was also a repository of Aryan virtues—physically strenuous, virile, forthright, and endowed with a vocal sense of "justice." Most important Roosevelt's progressivism was a politics of social harmony, not of strife. Ross was a preventive progressive. He wanted,

---

Chinese, p. 65. On collective farming, *Russia in Upheaval*, ch. 7, especially p. 138.

[42] *Seventy Years of It*, 111. Ross' two principal attempts at exposes of corporate "sinning" were *Sin and Society* and *Latter-Day Sinners and Saints* (New York, 1910). Theodore Roosevelt signed a preface, which Ross wrote, for *Sin and Society*, and the book sold remarkably well. Roosevelt to Ross, September 12, 1907 and an undated draft of a letter from Ross to Roosevelt, ca. September 1, 1907. On the Stanford affair, see *Seventy Years of It*, ch. 7, where a number of key documents of the firing are reprinted; numerous newspaper clippings on the incident in the Ross papers; Ross to Mrs. Beach, November 28, 1897; memorandum, David Starr Jordan to Ross, April 8, 1897.

more than anything else, social peace, an end to the contest of class against class. For a few of his contemporaries, Bolshevism seemed to hold out the best hope for community, but Ross was repelled by Bolshevism because it set one class against another and hence, inevitably, contributed to the binding of the individual by a collective will. Ross actually wanted (and he never realized the irony of it) to prevent *Social Control* from coming true, to preserve the individual against the community by salvaging an economic environment in which the individual could function. Roosevelt offered a way between the abuses of corporate capitalism and Bolshevism.[43]

Ross also devoted vigorous political efforts toward closing the gates of immigration. He could not reopen the frontier, much as he would have liked to, but he did try to keep out the Slavs, Italians, Chinese, and Japanese who were hemming in the individualistic Anglo-Saxon. He wanted desperately to keep the "sub-normal and low-grade people shut up in their own country." So he joined the effort to prevail on Woodrow Wilson to preserve as much as was left of the nation's purity. "There ought," he wrote to Wilson,

> to be on guard at the Nation's gates a man whose family line is entwined with the national past, and feels a normal American reaction at the spectacle of this country being held back by the constant pouring in of immigrants from progressively lower social grades and from peoples more remote from the orbit of our civilization.

Ross was haunted by "mongrelism" and "race suicide." "Anglo-Saxon" and "American" were metaphors for "individual" and "freedom." The irony, again, is that Ross hoped to blot out a historical fact which had dictated entire chapters of *Social Control,* the *Foundations of Sociology,* and *Social Psychology.*[44]

---

[43] On Roosevelt, see *Seventy Years of It,* pp. 245-247; the preface to *Sin and Society;* Roosevelt to Ross, June 15, 1906, December 12, 1914; Ross to Roosevelt, November 13, 1915. On Bolshevism, Ross' Russian notebook number 3, pp. 88-89, in Ross papers.

[44] Ross' most important anti-immigration statements were in *The Old World in the New* (New York, 1914), *Changing America,* especially pp. 96-97, and *Foundations of Sociology,* p. 393. Ross to Woodrow Wilson, November 19, 1912; Ross to Roger W. Babson, a eugenicist, November 21, 1917. For Ross' racial attitudes, see *Social Control,* pp. 439-440; *Foundations of Sociology,* ch. 11; *Social Psychology,* p. 88. In the 1930s he recanted and confessed that his earlier racism had been a major error. *Seventy Years of It,* pp. 275-279.

The manifold ironies of Ross' career after 1900 do not mean that *Social Control* was written somewhere on the periphery of his mind and that, at heart, he was secretly committed to individualism all the while. They mean, instead, that his life was dominated, before and after *Social Control*, by the tension between individual and community, the same tension that in different forms directed the intellectual careers of Peirce and Baldwin. Peirce's statement of the ideal of community was radical and unalloyed by any nostalgia for the free, self-sufficient individual, and it was as nearly unique as it was radical. Ross' critique of individualism was grudging and incomplete. For him, community was more a reluctantly acknowledged necessity than an ideal, a necessity evaded in practice almost as soon as it was surrendered to in theory. Peirce and Ross stood, in short, at opposite poles, but the polarity lay entirely within the conceptual quest for community. Both their intellectual lives were controlled by the same recognition—the individual, in the world of industrial capitalism and of the "tangled bank" of biology, was a helpless cipher. The quality of the recognition was markedly different, but the most essential facts were the same. In fact, paradoxically, Ross illustrates the compelling strength of the demand for a social concept of man even better than Peirce, for Ross reluctantly became a partisan of community against very strong promptings of predilection and personal history.

Chapter 5

Granville Stanley Hall: The Genetic Community

Granville Stanley Hall, eminent psychologist and president of Clark University, publicly claimed that he sometimes took off his clothes and rolled in the grass. He went home on regular visits to the farm country in western Massachusetts where he had grown up and systematically tried to recover some of the joyous abandon which, in middle age, he attributed to his youth. Gradually, during the summer, he would shed hat and tie, then coat, vest, shirt, collar, shoes, and stockings. Then he would climax solitary hill-climbing excursions by stripping off the rest of his clothes and falling to earth, "feeling pricked, caressed, bitten and stung all over, reverting to savagery as I had often done as a boy by putting off civilization with all clothes and their philosophy." Hall cultivated the primitivist, pagan side of his work and his personality, and he was probably capable of inventing such stories about himself. Whether he did in fact ever roll naked on a New England hillside is irrelevant; he did tell the story. An intellectual, especially one as imaginative as Hall, sometimes construes his life as drama, performing or inventing a symbolic act that will sum up the wide range of memories, ideas, and ideals that compose his experience. Stripping and rolling in the grass, either in fact or in imagination, was a metaphorical way of capturing and fixing for review an elusive mental world jumbled with variety and apparent inconsistency. The metaphor reduced his world to its simplest elements—civilization, clothes, and "their philosophy" on one side and nakedness, savagery, and sensuality on the other. The tense dichotomy showed plain, and the possibility of shed-

114

ding civilization and recovering savagery for once took concrete and active form.[1]

Hall needed the simplicity of the metaphor to lend precision and clarity to some very vague and confused ideas. Clothes were a simple sign for a long, complex inventory of the ills of civilization—sophistication and sin; loss of physical vigor; impersonal, hard cities where virtue and identity were wrecked; factories with their dehumanizing division of labor; premature mental and physical old age; bookishness and over-schooling; mistreatment of primitive peoples by imperial powers, and an overweening emphasis on intellect, consciousness, and self-consciousness. The "savagery" of nakedness condensed a similarly long and confused list of opposing values—naivete and innocence; health; farm life, and the close, personal relations of a New England town in the mid-nineteenth century; domestic industries in which all the procedures were common knowledge; youth; fondness for primitive peoples, in fact for primitivism in almost any form, and the primacy of instinct, feeling, and sense over the refinements of consciousness and intellect. These two sets of notions, in a welter of different guises, threaded their way through every year of Hall's mature career as a psychologist, university administrator, social philosopher, and publicist. The opposition between them was one of the controlling facts of his intellectual life. His psychological research, his educational programs, his attitudes toward social problems were all designed to promote the recovery of preindustrial virtue.

Hall's clue to a mechanism of recovery was the evolutionary theory of recapitulation. He believed, much more firmly than Baldwin did, that each individual passed through, in brief, all the evolutionary stages traversed by the species, that ontogeny recapitulated phylogeny. Every animal, therefore, was a compound of racial form and individual differences. In man the difficulty was that the "over-refinements" of civilization created an alarming gap between the private man and the "racial soul," between the individual soul and the collective entity that Hall named variously the race, humanity, mankind, or "Mansoul."

---

[1] Hall, "Note on Early Memories," *Pedagogical Seminary*, 6(1899), reprinted in Hall, *Recreations of a Psychologist* (New York, 1920), pp. 324-325.

Mansoul was Hall's synonym for what Peirce, Ross, and Baldwin called community or society, and in Hall the quest for community took the form of a quest for reunion between men and Mansoul, between the individual and the race.[2]

Hall's evolutionary psychology, like Baldwin's social psychology, Ross' sociology or Peirce's logic, was a vehicle for ethics, a program for good conduct. "The whole of morality," Hall thought, "may be well-defined as life in the interest of the race." The individual, cut off from the race, was ethically incomplete. Only by shedding selfish individual motives, by acting always and wholly in the interests of the race, could a man become genuinely ethical. Individual consciousness was artificial, housing only the "topmost twigs of the buried tree of mind." The individual man was a mere "fragment broken off from the great world of soul," and the highest task of life was to uncover the "buried tree," to recover membership in the "great cosmos of Soul":

> Ideal conduct is that which first developes the individual and then subordinates it to the race. . . . Just as far as we owe what we are to the long line of ancestors from whom our life is derived, so the interests of posterity should be the highest, most pervasive, and most controlling ethical motive.

This was, or so Hall claimed, a thoroughly naturalistic ethical program. He rejected the conventional religious grounding for ethics when he stopped training for the ministry, and his subsequent commitment to a physiological concept of mind prevented him from accepting the private morality of transcendental "conscience." There remained to him an abiding faith in evolution, and he made an evolving collective, the race, the substitute for God and the measure of conduct. Service to the race was man's chief end, and the source of all sin was the exaltation of individual wants and needs over the welfare of the collective Mansoul.[3]

In the child and particularly in the adolescent, Hall believed, the gulf between individual and race was narrowest. While the

---

[2] Strickland, "The Child and the Race," discusses at some length Hall's scheme of recapitulation. For a clear statement of Hall's commitment to the idea, see his *Adolescence, Its Psychology and Its Relations to Physiology, Anthropology, Sociology, Sex, Crime, Religion and Education* (Two volumes, New York, 1904), I, pp. 1-3.

[3] *Ibid.*, II, pp. 66, 69, 139, 304; Hall, *Jesus, the Christ in the Light of Psychology* (Two volumes, New York, 1917), II, p. 368.

drama of recapitulation was being played out, the evolutionary thrust was strongest, the needs of the race uppermost, and the selfish motives of the individual weakest. The natural outcome of a normal adolescence was the desire to serve, to abridge the self on behalf of the race as a whole. Adolescence was man's best hour, youth "the golden age of life, the child the consummate flower of creation, and most of all things worthy of love, reverence and study." Like Baldwin, Hall used child study as a medium for social philosophy and, again like Baldwin, made initiation into the community the pivotal event of youth.[4]

Such a conception of childhood, which Hall reached in his thirties and forties, lent peculiar importance to his view of his own youth. The picture Hall painted of himself rolling naked on a hillside was only the climactic scene in a much more elaborate recreation of his boyhood. He never cut himself loose from childhood despite many years of European travel and study, two marriages, a distinguished professorship, and thirty years as a university president with an international reputation. When the old family farm was being sold off in the 1890s, Hall bought the central 135 acres and held onto them with what he called "great piety." He visited the graves of his parents every summer and planned, toward the end of his life, to be buried alongside them in the village cemetery. In the 1880s, when he was gaining middle-aged academic success, Hall systematically began to reconstruct what he called his "boy life." He interviewed old inhabitants of the town of Ashfield, compiled a history of the town, mapped out the original farms after a painstaking study of old stone walls, visited the farmhouses where he had lived as a boy in an effort to evoke as many memories as possible, and even collected clothes, tools, and other artifacts to form a small museum in the basement of his old school.[5]

The result of this systematic revisitation was a highly stylized vision of an "earthly paradise" in the Berkshire hills of western Massachusetts. Hall recovered from the locale enough pleasant

---

[4] *Adolescence*, chs. 11, 14, especially p. 304.

[5] "Boy Life in a Massachusetts Country Town Thirty Years Ago," a paper Hall read before the American Antiquarian Society at Worcester, October 21, 1890, and published for the first time in the society's *Proceedings*, n.s. 7(1891), p. 107; "Note on Early Memories," pp. 297, 323; Hall, *Life and Confessions of a Psychologist* (New York, 1923), p. 53.

memories to construct an imaginative picture of the "best educational environment for boys . . . ever realized in history." His
version of boy life in the towns of Ashfield and Worthington in
the 1850s was a self-contained model of primitive virtues. Men
and boys lived close to nature in intimate familiarity with stream-
beds and trees, farm animals and smaller wild game. Every
member of the family participated in the chores and home industries that sustained the simple life. Morality was unambiguous, firmly rooted in the "ideal hearth and fireplace of olden
times," and clearly understood in "the simple virtues of industry,
frugality and clean living." Social relationships were straightfor-
ward, built on easy, face-to-face daily contact. A child in such
surroundings recapitulated the beginnings of civilization with a
fluency unsurpassed in any other culture and went easily "back to
sources, and made contact with the fresh primary thought, beliefs, feelings, and modes of life of the race, or of simple, homely,
genuine, primitive men." Adolescence in this environment went
its spontaneous way, reaching its natural culmination unimpeded
by the "artificialities" of city life, factory labor, or precocious
sophistication. "Ontogeny," Hall proudly claimed, "did in a rather
rare sense recapitulate phylogeny."[6]

Hall took an important step beyond identifying New England
farm life with the primitive adolescence of the race. He also associated Ashfield in the 1850s with the virtuous, eighteenth-century
childhood of America in the same way that Ross attributed
healthy republican virtues to his Iowa. In the isolated New England town of mid-century, he believed, a boy got "the same training that the heroes of '76 had." The effective equality of all
families, the easy familiarity of the citizens with one another, the
atmosphere of frugal, modest competence—these were the conditions of life and liberty that had been the cherished assumptions
of the authors of independence and the Constitution: "This mode
of life is the one and the only one that represents the ideal basis
of a state of citizen voters as contemplated by the framers of our
institutions." But the gently drawn portrait of Ashfield was also
an elegy on the "lamented decay" of New England farm life.

---

[6] "Boy Life in a Massachusetts Country Town," pp. 108, 120; *Life and Confessions,* 144-146; "Note on Early Memories," pp. 307, 314.

Hall's reconstruction of his youth got dramatic tension from his realization that the innocent virtues he attributed to Ashfield at mid-century had passed "beyond the reach of record." Indeed, he published his first account of "boy life" in the journal of the American Antiquarian Society, an organization devoted to the preservation of memories. Hall knew it was already too late to salvage anything but memories and relics. Preparing a museum of old clothes and tools was merely acknowledging the disappearance of an entire style of life and a consequent transformation of values.[7]

The basic agency of change, he thought, was technology. Machinery and artificial fertilizers had radically damaged farming technique and domestic industries and had altered the intimate likeness of farm life to the adolescence of man. Technology had driven an artificial wedge between men and their sustenance, and, as a result, the people had lost the robust vitality and homely virtue he claimed to remember from an earlier generation:

> The women are haggard, the men sometimes shiftless; and children are very rare. The heart of these communities is gone out of it [*sic*], and only the shell remains. . . . I know of nothing more sad in our American life than the decay of these townlets.

The lament was not only for Ashfield, but for America at large. Ashfield's decay was only a microcosmic representation of the industrial transformation of American life. America, like every New England "townlet," had caught civilization, a disease very dangerous to innocence and vitality. Civilization bred factories and cities, which assaulted men in the same insidious ways that farm machinery and artificial fertilizers spoiled the idyllic quality of life in Ashfield. Urban and industrial life brought with it all the evils of old age and choked off the naive vitality of youth. Life in the city was sedentary and so soiled with bad air and poor light that men did not even grow to full height. The factories fractured work into so many stages that workers had no idea how a whole shirt or shoe was made. Motor skills, the precious inheritance from primitive man, lapsed entirely. Morally, Hall believed, urban life caused precocious puberty, temptation, and

---

7 "Boy Life in a Massachusetts Country Town," p. 108; Hall, *Aspects of Child Life and Education* (Boston, 1907), viii.

vice and had none of the protective "sanifying influence and repose of nature" of the country. Modern cities were only great
"biological furnaces in which life is consumed."[8]

A city or a factory anywhere in the world was dangerous
enough, but in America industrialization was peculiarly evil.
America had not had a proper youth. It had passed in too short
a time from a precious rural childhood into premature old age.
Its heroes, even, were all gray sages. Immigrants, who composed
such an alarmingly large proportion of the population, came all
too often in their middle years. The native stock was growing
"senescent," abandoning its farms for the city, and producing too
few children. "No country," Hall fretted, "is so precociously old."
And a precocious country exposed itself just as much as a precocious adolescent to the great danger of dementia praecox. Hall
was afraid that the forced pace of maturity and the predominance
of cities and great industries would bring on the dread symptoms
of precocious dementia—withdrawal and morbid self-consciousness. Youth, either in a nation or an individual, was pregnant with
great moral possibility, but youth needed romance, "idealization,"
and repose. In modern America there was neither repose nor
ideals, but only "hyper-sophistication" and "hyper-individuation."
In the "hothouse" of city and factory all the causes of dementia
praecox flourished—overwork and physical exhaustion for the
children of the poor and early "ripening" for the children of the
rich. The temptations of city life encouraged the greatest cause
of the disease, premature sexual experience. "Forbidden pleasures
are tasted, till the soul has sometimes not only lost its innocence
. . . but life is blase, a burnt-out cinder."[9]

The symptoms of dementia praecox, the turning inward, the
chronic concern with the self, were perfectly opposed to the selfless morality Hall wanted to encourage. The Edenic vision of life
on the farm in Ashfield was his metaphorical cure for the disease.
The historical accuracy of his description of his "boy life" was
not important; indeed, he probably was unhappy in his actual
childhood. What he created was a medium for criticism, and the
technique was more literary than historical. The idyllic vision

---

[8] "Boy Life in a Massachusetts Country Town," 126; *Adolescence,* I, pp. 30,
166, 169, 172, 321 ff., II, p. 747.
[9] *Ibid.,* I, viii, xv, pp. 321-322.

provided a nostalgic contrast, much like Edward Bellamy's Boston of the year 2000 or Henry Adams' rendering of the thirteenth century in *Mont-Saint-Michel and Chartres*, a metaphorical vehicle for the somewhat gloomy judgment Hall wanted to pass on American industrial capitalism.[10]

The criticism was not only of America; it was also Hall's commentary on the way that he, like America, was cut off from Ashfield. Like Ross, Hall left his farm and village for Europe and for academic success and reputation. In Hall's case the break with home was an even greater psychological wrench. He was much more deeply rooted in western Massachusetts than Ross was in Iowa. The Halls had been in Massachusetts since John Winthrop led the Puritans over from England in 1630, and he could trace his mother's ancestry to John Alden. The first Hall settled in Ashfield in 1780, and he claimed that seven generations of the family had lived on the same land. One-fourth of Ashfield's population was named Hall, and as many others were relatives. Hall's father had been tempted by Wisconsin, but after only a brief stay had come home to settle in the Berkshires. The family was bound to Ashfield and the surrounding country by every tie of history and blood, and any Hall was assured of a confident identity.[11]

The life Hall encountered outside Ashfield was entirely different. The "dominantly sad note" of his life was personal isolation, totally unlike the happy sense of natural community he claimed had existed in Ashfield. His parents heightened the isolation and discontinuity by refusing to leave Ashfield to visit him at Harvard or Johns Hopkins. If he wanted to relieve his isolation and renew family life, Hall had to go back to Ashfield. Marriage might have helped resolve the problem, but both of his marriages were broken. His first wife died in an accident in 1890, and his second became unmanageably insane shortly after their marriage and had to be committed to a sanitarium. Hall's encounter with the world outside Ashfield was successful professionally, but despite the

---

[10] For examples of Hall's very rare adverse judgments on his actual childhood, see *Life and Confessions*, pp. 176, 594. Hall's reconstruction of childhood reeks of false hope, and his homage to his parents reeks just as much of guilt at having deserted the "ideal hearth." *Ibid.*, especially pp. 83-85.

[11] *Ibid.*, pp. 22, 24, 53, 61-62, 81, 144.

success, he was dogged almost as much as Peirce by the sense of isolation. His reconstruction of life in Ashfield made the extent of his break with his family and youth unmistakably clear. Ashfield was a model of a society to which Hall could feel he had thoroughly belonged, with membership rights that were not open to question. Ashfield was, in fact, a working model of Mansoul, and the ideal of Mansoul was a potent theoretical antidote to Hall's own itineracy.[12]

In 1862, when he was eighteen, Hall put an end to his adolescence and to life in Ashfield and went off to Williston Seminary at Easthampton, Massachusetts, to prepare for college. The family struggle over whether he should go to college was severe, but Hall and his mother won out, so after a year at Williston Seminary, he walked to Williamstown to apply for entrance to Williams College. At Williams, where he was ostensibly preparing for the ministry, Hall got a standard mid-century education, founded on Greek, Latin, and mathematics and capped by a thoroughly Christian training in moral philosophy at the hands of President Mark Hopkins. There were a few excursions outside orthodoxy. On the prompting of John Bascom, Hall learned something of John Stuart Mill, and a visit to Williamstown by Emerson (still considered too radical to speak on the college grounds) set Hall to reading the Concord philosophy. But the main business of the college was religion. Hopkins' course was accompanied by carefully timed prayer meetings led by his brother, Albert Hopkins, and every young man was extensively prayed over until he showed evidence of conversion. During the regular spring revival of his sophomore year, Hall acknowledged his conviction of sin and took the regular steps to conversion and membership in the college church. For the next two years he participated in the organized religious activities of the college and walked three miles every Sunday to lead a Bible class for the "mature women" of the village of Blackington.[13]

After he graduated from Williams, Hall went to New York to enter another bastion of orthodoxy, Union Theological Seminary.

[12] *Life and Confessions*, pp. 75, 594-595; Lorine Pruett, *G. Stanley Hall: a Biography of a Mind* (New York, 1926), pp. 95-96; Edward L. Thorndike, "Granville Stanley Hall, 1846-1924," *Biographical Memoirs of the National Academy of Sciences*, 12(1929), p. 135.
[13] *Life and Confessions*, pp. 151-172.

He took the regular courses in New Testament, church history, homiletics, and pastoral theology. To get practical experience and fifty cents a day in wages, he visited tenement families and tried to coax prostitutes into mission prayer meetings. Like all the candidates for the ministry, he prepared a trial sermon, and toward the end of the year he was sent to take a pulpit in the little Pennsylvania town of Coudersport.[14]

His commitment to orthodoxy was already weak. During college vacations he had fallen under the liberal influence of Charles Eliot Norton, who spent his summers in Ashfield. Norton had cast the spell of Dante, Carlyle, and John Ruskin over Hall. Then had come Hall's preoccupation with Mill and Emerson. The reading followed no particular pattern, but it did challenge the limits of thought so carefully drawn by Mark Hopkins and Hall's own pious and conservative family. In New York Hall joined the Brooklyn church of the famous and mildly liberal Henry Ward Beecher, and he assiduously followed the sermons and lectures of the most radical Unitarian of them all, Octavius Brooks Frothingham. Beecher and Frothingham alone would probably have caused only a modest veering from the theology Hall learned at Union—just enough to make the president of the seminary pray over Hall that he might be returned to orthodoxy—but Hall exposed himself to every kind of stimulus. He went to hear debates at the Cooper Union, where all kinds of questions and views were aired, and he joined a small Positivist Club, where he studied August Comte and heard Darwin and Spencer taught by John Fiske.[15]

Most of all, however, it was the city that stimulated and provoked a young seminarian fresh from the farm and a narrow college. Hall luxuriated in the novelty and variety of New York. He attended the services of every church and sect. He taught history in a fashionable private school for girls. He visited mediums and phrenologists, watched great fires, attended police courts, went to morgues and foundling homes. He was captivated by the theater, the Shakespeare of Edwin Booth and the opera of Offenbach, and he joined the Philharmonic chorus. Everything was new and exciting to Hall, who had never been to a town

[14] *Life and Confessions,* pp. 177-179, 182.
[15] *Ibid.,* pp. 179-181.

as large as nearby Springfield, and after the experience in New York, preaching sermons and presiding over occasional funerals in Coudersport was bound to be intolerable. Hall took the first opportunity to escape. After he had been at Coudersport for nine weeks, a letter arrived from Beecher. It was addressed to Hall in New York and merely asked him to call, but Hall took the earliest train to the city and went at once to Brooklyn Heights. Beecher gave him the release he wanted. He prevailed on a wealthy member of the congregation to lend Hall $1,000 to finance study in Germany. Hall had no confidence that he could face his family with the news, so he sailed the next day for Europe.[16]

He spent the next thirteen years in desultory groping for a subject matter and a career, and by the time he settled into a job at Johns Hopkins and into psychology and "pedagogy" as a discipline, he was thirty-eight years old. What he called his first "triennium" in Germany, from 1868-1872, was passed in undecisive sampling. At Bonn and at Berlin, he hopefully took courses in theology. In fact J. A. Dorner's lectures at Berlin were the central intellectual event of these German years. Dorner held out the hope of a mediating theology that could reconcile orthodoxy with the radicalism of Hegel and Schleiermacher. Such a theology could have resolved Hall's vocational problem, for he was still interested in the ministry. When he returned to New York and took a tutoring job in the family of a banker, Jesse Seligman, Hall still went to the Seminary to hear lectures. And in his first academic job at Antioch College he conducted church services for the students from time to time and preached occasionally in the Unitarian church in Cincinnati. Before 1875, at least, the ministry or a teaching job with ministerial trappings was still his most distinct vocational possibility.[17]

All the while, Hall was casting about for another career. During his first German stay, he read Hegel assiduously and probed Aristotle and Kant in the seminar of the great Aristotelean, Trendelenberg. He frequented the lectures of Heinrich von Treitschke and sought out von Hartmann. Hall succeeded, or fancied he did,

---

[16] *Life and Confessions,* pp. 180-181.
[17] See the essay on Dorner in Hall, *Founders of Modern Psychology* (New York, 1912); *Life and Confessions,* pp. 186-203.

where Ross had pronounced himself a failure. He understood Hegel and some of the post-Hegelian idealists, and he could read someone like von Hartmann without getting rattled. Secular and speculative philosophy was an alternative to theology, and Hall was prepared to help introduce this German subject matter into America. In the years between his first and second trips to Germany Hall wrote on Dorner for the *Presbyterian Quarterly*, but he also discussed Hegel for the *Journal of Speculative Philosophy* and translated Karl Rosenkranz's *Hegel as the National Philosopher of Germany*.[18]

Hall also succeeded in liking Germany and enjoying his years there. He made friends where Ross had not, and he lived intimately in a German family. Perhaps most important, he went to Germany already prepared by a year of exploring in New York, so he was not nearly so shocked by Berlin as Ross was when he confronted the city directly from Fort Dodge. But an affinity for Germany and German philosophy, though they might supply a kind of intellectual identity, could by no means solve the problem of a career for Hall, and when he came home in the spring of 1871, he simply had no job. He tutored the Seligman children for about a year and then was offered an instructorship at Antioch. But his work at Antioch, like Ross' at the Fort Dodge Collegiate Institute, did not create an intellectual career. His subjects were almost as various as Ross'—English, German literature, French literature, and philosophy. He was simultaneously an enthusiastic Spencerian and Hegelian, but he had no real discipline. The teaching amounted only to more education, and Antioch was only a slightly better stage than the pulpit at Coudersport.[19]

---

[18] "Outline of Dr. J. A. Dorner's System of Theology," *Presbyterian Quarterly*, n.s. 1(1872), pp. 720-747, 2(1873), pp. 60-93, 267-273; the translation of Rosenkranz, with whom Hall studied in Germany, was published in St. Louis in 1874; Hall, "Note on Hegel and his Critics," *Journal of Speculative Philosophy*, 12(1878), pp. 93-103; *Life and Confessions*, pp. 190-193. On Hall's early reaction to von Hartmann, see Hall, "Hartmann's New System of Pessimistic Ethics," in *Aspects of German Culture* (Boston, 1881), pp. 175-185.

[19] *Life and Confessions*, pp. 188-189, 196-203. Compare Hall's good-natured attitude toward Germany and Europe, exhibited in letters home to the *Nation*, collected in *Aspects of German Culture*, with Ross' Berlin diary or his homecoming essay, "Turning Toward Nirvana."

He was waiting for a summons again, and this time the role of
Beecher's forwarded letter was played by the first volume of
Wundt's *Physiological Psychology*. Hall read it and resigned
almost at once to go back to Germany. The passage to Berlin
detoured through Cambridge, Massachusetts, where he spent two
years teaching the sophomore English survey course at Harvard.
But he made good use of the two years to get a head start on
physiology and psychology. In the time he could steal from teaching at Harvard he wrote a dissertation on "The Muscular Perception of Space" for a Ph.D. He was thirty-four, but at last he
had a subject.[20]

Hall spent two years at Leipzig and Berlin, studying with
Wundt, Helmholtz, DuBois-Reymond, Carl Ludwig, who was
Wundt's equal in experimental physiology, and other physiolo-
gists and psychologists. His commitment to his new discipline
deepened with work. He was still interested in philosophy, but
he was convinced now that psychology and physiology could
lead speculation to earth, make it more critical and so more fruitful. This would be his vocation. He came home in 1880, a Ph.D.
with five years of German training, four years of college teaching
experience, debts, and a pregnant wife. He was thirty-six and
ready to make his mark. But once more he had no job, and he
took a small apartment just outside Cambridge to wait. Harvard,
in the person of President Charles William Eliot, came to his
rescue. Eliot invited him to give a series of public lectures on
pedagogy and a small course in contemporary German philosophy
in the university. The decision to use the public lectures to apply
what he had learned of psychology to the somewhat uncertain
science of pedagogy was made, Hall claimed, with an eye only
to "making bread." In any case the decision brought him almost
immediate success. Eliot helped attract attention to the lectures,
and the newspapers reported them favorably. Hall was asked to
give the series in Baltimore in 1881, and the next year he was invited to take his first real university job at Johns Hopkins. He
moved into a house across the street from Peirce, set up a laboratory, founded the *American Journal of Psychology*, and began

---

[20] See "The Muscular Perception of Space," *Mind* 3(1878), pp. 433-450.
Hall remembered 1880 or 1881 as the date of his Ph.D., but it was 1878.
Life and Confessions, p. 119; Thorndike, "G. Stanley Hall," p. 136.

to write. Within a few years, his long apprenticeship was over and he was a pronounced academic success.[21]

Hall's career after 1882 bore a striking resemblance to Baldwin's. Both men began in the laboratory with a professional commitment to experiment. But Hall, like Baldwin, soon found that the microscope and the stop watch held no answers to the kinds of questions he had in mind. In the 1880s and 1890s he devoted more and more of his time and energy to pedagogy and child study and gradually abandoned laboratory physiology. His interest in the child was not so much experimental as ethical. He attempted some uncontrolled observations of his own; he worked out a questionnaire technique for gathering statistical information on children, and he reported at length on the statistical results of European child study. But observation and the compilation of statistics could no more satisfy Hall than Baldwin. Hall was a moral philosopher in the tradition of Mark Hopkins, and he used child psychology, especially after 1890, as a vehicle for moralizing. Finally, after the turn of the century, even the formal limitations of child psychology were too constraining, and Hall followed Baldwin's path into speculative religious philosophy.[22]

In the 1870s Hall had actively sought a discipline, and when Wundt's *Physiological Psychology* appeared, he had pounced on the chance to identify himself with a concrete subject matter. The discipline promised to give focus to his diffuse intellectual interests, and, at the same time, it had created an institutional identity. Having a subject meant having a vocation, a university chair, official membership in an institutional community, and po-

---

[21] Hall's pedagogical lectures were expansions of the ideas of "The Moral and Religious Training of Children," *Princeton Quarterly*, 10(1882), pp. 26-48. *Life and Confessions*, pp. 204-224; *Adolescence*, I, pp. 129-130; Eliot's introduction to the lectures is reprinted in Hall, *Educational Problems* (Two volumes, New York, 1911), II, p. 241.

[22] For examples of Hall's laboratory work, see "Optical Illusions of Motion," *Journal of Physiology*, 3(1882), pp. 297-307, or "Dermal Sensitiveness to Gradual Pressure Changes," *American Journal of Psychology*, 1(1887), pp. 72-98. Hall's best-known observational study was "The Story of a Sand Pile," first published in *Scribner's* in 1888 and reprinted in *Aspects of Child Life and Education*, pp. 142-156. His most influential effort at reporting European findings, with a slight mixture of his own results, was "The Contents of Children's Minds," first published in 1883 and also reprinted in *Ibid.*, pp. 1-52. For a good example of Hall's commitment to physiology, see his glowing review of George Trumbull Ladd, *Elements of Physiological Psychology*, *American Journal of Psychology*, 1(1887), pp. 159-164.

tential recovery of the kind of sure identity he had left behind in Ashfield. To be "professor of psychology and pedagogy" at Johns Hopkins was something like being "Hall" in Ashfield. The sense of identity was heightened still further in 1889, when Hall became president of the new Clark University. He also founded four professional journals, expanding his intellectual patrimony just as his ancestors had added to the family acreage. And, as if the university presidency and the journals were not enough, Hall always insisted on his membership in a movement, a "new psychology" and a "new pedagogy," proud of the advance of his intellectual phalanx. In the end Hall's glum estimate of his life as one of continuous "isolation" belied any confidence of membership, but even a veneer of institutional security and academic reputation was enough to release him from the laboratory. The accumulation of professional honors made it possible to explore with increasing abandon, and, especially after 1900, his intellectual style was one of self-assertion and pronouncement.[23]

Hall's transformation from a would-be scientist into a self-conscious prophet and social philosopher hinged on the pivotal experiences of the last half of the decade of the 1880s. His appointment to the Clark presidency signaled success, but the gain was balanced by profound losses. His father died in 1885 and his mother two years later. Family life in Ashfield was only a cluster of memories. Then, three years later, his wife and daughter were killed by escaping gas in the family's new home in Worcester. A fire which destroyed the buildings on the Ashfield farm seemed only to ratify the losses. "I felt," he remembered later, "that a retreat in possible disaster was cut off, and that I had only then landed high and dry on the hither side of my Rubicon." Simultaneously, in the space of five swift years, Hall had gained a new eminence from which to survey the world and make pronounce-

---

[23] The journals, which exemplified the expansion of Hall's interests, were *The American Journal of Psychology* (1887), *The Pedagogical Seminary* (1893), *The Journal of Religious Psychology* (1904, suspended in 1917), and *The Journal of Applied Psychology* (1917). On the "new" psychology and pedagogy, see Hall's extensive review of books by Dewey, McCosh, and Borden P. Bowen, *American Journal of Psychology,* 1(1887), pp. 146-159; "The New Psychology," Hall's inaugural lecture at Johns Hopkins, in *Andover Review,* 3(1885), pp. 120-135, 239-248; "New Departures in Education," *North American Review,* 140(1885), pp. 144-152.

ments on its state and had lost most of the family associated with his younger life. He spent the next ten years transferring the sense of loss to America and devising a psychological mechanism of recovery, not only for himself but for his country.[24]

Everywhere he looked after the mid-1880s Hall saw loss of youth and innocence. When he observed children playing in a sandpile over the course of several summers, he regretted the increasing "sophistication" of their games. In the beginning the sandpile was a simple arrangement, centered on a model Jeffersonian community. Then, in a striking parallel to Hall's version of the American experience, the "golden age of this little republic" ended, and the sandpile entered on a "period of over-refinement and ennervating luxury." After his parents died, Hall began the painstaking task of imaginatively reconstructing his "boy life," the golden age of his own little republic of Ashfield and Worthington. He projected the radical changes in his own life into the transformation of American society, and he fretted about the ability of America to meet the challenges of industrialism and the city:

> Once the typical citizen was the independent small farmer . . . alert, intelligent, intensely interested in all public affairs, with considerable time for reading, debating, and town meeting. He was honest, fearless, pious, and industrious, his own master. . . . Now, the majority of our citizens are urban. They are employees working for wages . . . with no schooling on the average beyond the sixth grade. . . . Most of them have been here only a generation or two and know little of the spirit and traditions of their adopted country. . . . They need to be taught patriotism, integrity, honesty, hygiene and of this they get but little.

When Hall had come home in 1880 from his second stay in Germany, he had been struck by the predominance of "business" in American life, but then he had been confident of the general good health of his country. Twenty years later, he was afraid that the city and the factory would totally destroy the virtues he thought had nurtured his New England ancestors.[25]

Gradually, Hall's conception of the problem of American life focused on the excess of individualism, and his social philosophy

[24] *Life and Confessions*, pp. 224, 253; Pruett, *G. Stanley Hall*, pp. 95-96.
[25] "The Story of a Sandpile," p. 153; "First Impressions on Returning from Germany," *Aspects of German Culture*, pp. 304-320; *Educational Problems*, II, p. 626.

took form around the polar opposites of self-seeking and service. Like Peirce, Baldwin, and Ross, he concluded that America was faced with a crucial choice between uncontrolled individual avarice and service to the collective needs of the community. The Pullman strike of 1894, he thought, revealed in capsule the basic flaw of American capitalism. The strike forced the question "What do we need in this country today, what do these men who are rioting in Chicago . . . need?" The pastoral life of a New England town was no viable antidote to the industrial disease. Even Hall knew that Ashfield was gone beyond recovery. The answer must be found in a new morality. The rioters, he told the members of the National Education Association,

> need to take the altruistic standpoint, and show that the center of life is not self but others. When the struggle for the survival of the individual has given way to the higher struggle for the survival of others, inspirited by Christian sentiment, then will come a better civilization. . . . Life is for service; it is not for self, and this idea should be implanted deeply in the heart of every child.

It was easy enough to prescribe, to simply tell angry men not to be selfish. It was more difficult to elaborate grounds for such an ethic, to make it seem not only desirable but possible. Hall was fifty years old in the year of the Pullman strike, and he had not yet written a real book; but the challenge was compelling. He now had a cause, the quest for community, and the intensity of his hopes and fears seemed to gather up and release an immense amount of psychological energy. During the next thirty years, he ground out one immense book after another, each one devoted to searching out the cure for individualism.[26]

Hall's major books were sustained by a devout faith in cosmic evolution. He suffered and gained, in some of the same ways as Peirce, from the "monistic pathos." Peirce dreamed of "the unity of the body of all things," Hall of the "sense of unity and law at the root of things and pervading every action and corner of space." The philosophers he listened to most carefully—Emerson, John Fiske, Hegel, Spencer, von Hartmann—all were men of

[26] "Child Study," National Education Association *Proceedings* (1894), 179.

cosmic vision, who saw in the universe what Hall thought of as "the unfoldment of a mighty process." The process, of course, was evolution, but Hall was incapable of the kind of tough, rigorously naturalistic rendering of evolution that a William Graham Sumner or a Chauncey Wright could produce. He could not read *The Origin of Species* as a biological account of a natural process. Instead, he clung to Darwin's sparse references to a Creator and to the rather apologetic conclusion of the later editions of *The Origin of Species* that "there is a grandeur in this view of life." Like Baldwin, Hall grasped at evolution as a cosmic process, a way to "conceive the whole world, material and spiritual, as an organic unity." In the first half of his life he shed a succession of gods—the God of his fathers and of Union Seminary, the milder God of the Unitarians and of Antioch, the cunning Reason of Hegel. But, rather than be altogether without, he deified the evolutionary process itself. Every natural fact, for Hall, was not a mere symbol of a spiritual fact; natural facts *were* spiritual facts, creations of the "divine logos," or "Bio-logos . . . the spirit of life that had brooded over the universe." Hall quickly chastised any man like William James who did not approach the universe with the appropriate "spirit of reverence" for a world that was "religious to the core."[27]

There could be no breach in such a universe, no dualism of nature and spirit or mind and matter. The "new psychology" to which Hall was so attached had to heal "all breaks and supernaturalism," to elaborate a conception of mind that would recover the continuous unity of reason and instinct, of human intellect and animal intelligence. "Soul," for Hall, was neither distinctly human nor private. Soul was "homogeneous and also continuous throughout the animal kingdom." From Descartes to Hegel, he claimed, prevailing conceptions of human nature had been severely "mentalistic," radically separating body and soul, mind and nature, ego and subject. The dualism had prompted the misguided efforts of Kant, the vagaries of Berkeley, and the

---

[27] Review of James' *Principles of Psychology*, in *American Journal of Psychology*, 3(1891), p. 590; "Discussion," National Education Association *Proceedings* (1902), p. 221; *Adolescence*, I, pp. 129-130; *Life and Confessions*, pp. 358-359.

scepticism of Hume. Hall thought that a "genetic" psychology
could heal the breach and establish the basic dictum that "Nature
and the mind have the same root."[28]

Such a program for psychology seemed to Hall to demand an
uncompromising rejection of individualism. The "old" psychology
was built around the illusion of a rational, individual self or soul.
Hall wanted to work what he called a Copernican revolution in
psychology, to dislodge the individual self from its arbitrary
resting place at the center of things. This, in turn, required a de-
thronement of reason, consciousness, and self-consciousness. Consciousness, Hall had to admit, was individual. But consciousness
was only a "wart" on the soul, and being self-conscious was a
process of loss, of forgetting, of "progressive ignorance . . . of the
great cosmos of soul." Individuality, then, was an artificial barrier to man's proper membership in the cosmic, collective Mansoul. The only way to pierce the barrier was to dip below the
threshold of consciousness, to recover or "remember" the inherited, instinctive endowments that marked man as a creature of the
Bio-logos. "The heart," Hall thought, "is the organ of the race,
while the intellect is only that of the individual," and the ultimate
goal of psychology and of life was "the true paradise of a restored
intuitive human nature." The individual, artificially insulated by
a rational self-consciousness, was only a tragically finite fragment.
But the "collective soul" which dwelt so deeply below consciousness was a whole and infinitely subtle summation of all the evolutionary experiences of Mansoul, an answer to every real question,
a warmly impulsive antidote to the sterility of individuality.[29]

---

[28] *Adolescence*, II, pp. 41-44, 55, 63, 67; *Life and Confessions*, p. 358. A
thoroughgoing naturalist, like Wright or Sumner, would have said that the
mind has a natural root, but, in Hall's careful wording, mind and nature
had the "same root," the "Bio-logos."
[29] Review of James' *Principles*, p. 590; Hall and F. H. Saunders, "Pity,"
American Journal of Psychology, 11(1900), p. 573; *Adolescence*, II, pp. 65-
70, 647; "A Glance at the Phyletic Background of Genetic Psychology,"
American Journal of Psychology, 19(1908), pp. 149-212. The great attraction of von Hartmann was that he made the unconscious the "transcendent,
mediatory, real principle," prior in every way to private, individual consciousness. *Founders of Modern Psychology*, p. 238. Freud, also, was extremely attractive, for the same reason—he made the most important processes
those which went on below consciousness. Hall believed that "the advent of
Freudianism marked the greatest epoch in the history of our science." *Life
and Confessions*, pp. 406-414.

It was within this context that adolescence assumed such a central importance for Hall. The preadolescent youth was a fully developed individual personality, recapitulating a long, "pigmoid" plateau across which the race had long ago passed. But the adolescent passed rapidly through the evolutionary stage in which man had first become truly human. In this precious period of life the "flood gates of heredity" opened wide. The adolescent was exquisitely attuned to the subconscious racial soul within. Life, Hall thought, "pivoted" in adolescence from an individual to a collective center. Life performed, in fact, the kind of Copernican revolution he wanted to accomplish in psychology.

> The . . . law of service and self-sacrifice begins to loom up. Henceforth the race, not the self, must become supreme. . . . The old consciousness is sloughed off, and the soul enters, more or less transformed, its mature, imago stage, to live for the race and not for self.

Adolescence was an initiation into the human community, and it was, above all, an ethical experience. In the 1400 pages of his massive *Adolescence* Hall discussed all the physical, especially the sexual, changes of adolescence. But a change in brain weight or an awakening sexual desire was significant only as a manifestation of the ethical triumph of the race over the individual. Maturity was not an organic affair, but an affair of the heart, and "no man has reached his ethical majority who would not die if the real interests of the community could thus be furthered."[30]

Hall always claimed that his analysis of adolescence was empirical and scientific, and he shuddered when any of his critics suggested that his methods were merely imaginative. There were, after all, his questionnaires and some laboratory results to support his incessant claim that he was a scientist. But a set of returns from a questionnaire or a table of data were always invitations to speculation, and Hall found the invitation more and more inviting. By the turn of the century the speculations had only the most tenuous connection with the data. There was a brief period in the 1870s and 1880s when he could write restrained reports of experiments or observations, but after his career climbed out of

---

[30] Hall was critical enough of his age to feel that almost no one reached such an ethical majority. He accounted for this by admitting that the race itself was still in its adolescence, just on the pivotal point between individual and community. *Jesus, the Christ,* II, p. 484. *Adolescence,* II, chs. 10-11, 14-15; pp. 70, 303, 331.

the laboratory, Hall always thought more in metaphor than in formula. He never really left the pulpit, and in the end he was making the same pronouncements he had been trained to make at Union Seminary. He thought of the "science of man" as a "gospel of love," of the psychologist as a "high priest of souls," and of the New Testament as "the world's chief textbook in psychology." He was, in short, still a kind of minister, and his fondest dream was to give Christianity a new and lasting expression in the language of evolutionary psychology. By the time he reached his sixties, Hall found that he could once more repeat the Apostles' Creed "with a fervent sentiment of conviction."[31]

Folk psychology was the device Hall used to join evolution and Christianity. The distinguishing talent of the psychologist, he thought, ought to be insight into "a collective, *Volks*, mass, crowd, group, herd or community soul." Cities, social classes, medieval guilds, even a mob could have a soul just as unitary and real as any individual personality. The "great races of mankind" all had souls, he thought, and above all these hovered "the soul of humanity itself," Mansoul. Finally, "back of" Mansoul, there was what Hall called the "cosmic soul," the *animus mundi*, the "all-father-mother," the Bio-logos. Each of these great "souls" was only what it had become. Like many evolutionists, Hall was also an historicist. His very self-conscious "genetic" point of view centered on the assumption that everything, an organism or a collective soul, was a living resume of its past. Folk myths, then, had an extraordinary significance, for they were all at least partial histories of the development of Mansoul. The Old and the New Testaments were by far the most complete and perceptive of the folk myths. Although they had been articulated by the Jews, they captured the most profound experiences and longings of humanity. Thus the Bible was an evolutionary document of supreme importance, for it plumbed the very depths of Mansoul, and since every individual recapitulated the past of Mansoul, the Bible was also a generalized account of all men's experiences. This conviction fell somewhat short of the standards of empirical science, but armed with it Hall worked out a very systematic, evolutionary rereading of scripture.[32]

---

[31] Review of James' *Principles*, p. 540; *Life and Confessions*, p. 436; *Jesus, the Christ*, I, xv, xviii.
[32] *Life and Confessions*, pp. 438-443; *Adolescence*, II, pp. 320-321, 360.

The Edenic myth, he claimed, represented the prehistoric gens, a stage in the evolution of the race in which the clan or tribe was the "supreme, all-absorbing unity," a stage represented in recapitulation by the youth at the dawn of adolescence. Adam was a symbol for the beginnings of racial adolescence, and temptation and the fall were a mythical history of the breakdown of tribal solidarity and the beginnings of selfish individualism. In the individual, temptation and the fall were perennially re-enacted in pubescent "self-abuse," the inevitable "premature exercise of the genetive powers." Mankind and the individual, after the fall, passed through the dreary period of excessive impurity and selfishness detailed in the Old Testament, but the Prophets announced a dawning sense of guilt, a longing to regain the lost paradise of selfless innocence. The accusing God of the Prophets was a metaphor for the original collective paradise, still living as a racial memory in the individual's subconscious.[33]

The superb climax of the Jewish rendering of the history of Mansoul was the life and death of Christ. In the incarnation, Mansoul returned from its unnatural exile into the heavens to dwell once more in man on earth. The crucifixion and resurrection were the result of Christ's decision to sacrifice his individual life to create a symbol through which men might recover communal immortality. Christ's life was the "consummation of adolescence," for he perfected the radical rejection of individuality and finitude, and his conception of the kingdom was the world's clearest statement of the ideal of a community of love. Christ's acts and his teachings all converged on one ethical doctrine, "The individual utterly subordinates himself to love and serve his fellow-man." In fact Christ had carried the insight further and had intuitively discovered the fundamental law of nature, the subjection of the individual organism to the life of its species. This first natural law was also the first moral law; "To break away from this law and set up for self violates nature and constitutes the bottom sin or disease in the world." Beginning from radically different premises and using different techniques, Hall and Peirce worked out similar readings of both evolution and scripture. Hall knew Peirce in Baltimore and was familiar with

[33] *Adolescence*, II, pp. 303, 333-338; *Jesus, the Christ,* I, pp. 282-284, II, 353, 371-483. Hall's conception of the gens was derived mainly from Emil Durkheim.

Peirce's essay on "evolutionary love," but Peirce had no perceptible influence on Hall's work. The two men were simply responding to the same kinds of intellectual and social challenges, and they devised the same readings of *The Origin of Species* and the New Testament.[34]

Hall had a much more ritualistic mind than Peirce, however, and he could not relent until he had discovered a physiological or a psychological analogue for all the major Christian doctrines. For the dualism of body and soul he substituted August Weismann's distinction between "soma" and "plasma." The soma was, in Hall's scheme, the individual body, the flesh, all the members and organs that lived temporarily for the sole purpose of providing a medium for the plasma, the germinal substance of the race. To live in sin was to live for the soma, or flesh, and masturbation was the paradigm sin, for it wasted the soul for the selfish pleasure of the body. The highest exercise of virtue was procreation, in which the individual totally "sacrificed" himself to the future of Mansoul. Conception was a "holy intoxication," a "sacred hour," a "beatitude," an "annunciation hour," when "the race is incarnated in the individual and remembers its lost paradise." Salvation, then, was the real nature of the pivoting of life in adolescence. Fragmentary, finite individuality was cast off, and the adolescent gained the immortality of membership in the infinite, collective Mansoul. "All men are born twice," Hall thought, "once as individuals and once as representatives of the species. . . . Late adolescence merges the lower into the higher, social self. . . . The transition is in fact the chief antithesis in all the human cosmos."[35]

Hall's almost pathetically mechanical analogies among psychology, biology, and Christianity provided a schematic unity for his world view. But more than a world view was at stake, for the scheme also justified Hall's conception of his vocation. Because the reconciliation of Darwin and Christ focused on the adolescent, anyone who ministered to the needs of adolescence performed a "holy function" in a "holy cause." Pedagogy was thus

---

[34] *Adolescence*, II, pp. 292-295, 333-338; *Jesus, the Christ*, I, xiv, xviii, pp. 282-284, II, pp. 354, 361-363, 367-368, 377. On Peirce, see *Life and Confessions*, p. 266; *Adolescence*, II, p. 136.

[35] *Ibid.*, I, p. 452, II, pp. 121-123; 293-294, 304; *Jesus, the Christ*, II, p. 484; *Senescence: the Last Half of Life* (New York, 1922), p. 255.

the supreme science, the highest "*calling*"; the schoolroom was "sacrosanct," and ought to be approached with a "spirit of consecration." To teach, to teach others to teach, to do research on the techniques of teaching, to administer a university, all were religious vocations—much more genuinely religious than preaching in the pulpit at Coudersport or Cincinnati. The thirty-two years Hall spent at Clark University were frustrating and disappointing. The founder, Jonas Clark, never fulfilled his promises, the faculty grumbled and deserted, and the university never matured into the rival of Johns Hopkins that Hall contemplated. But within Hall's world view, his career as a university president could be conceived as something vastly more interesting and important than a mediocre administrative tour. Clark, he could conclude, was not a mere institution at all. It was a manifestation of the "University Invisible," a "temple" of the "church of science," a "shrine."[36]

The schools, Hall claimed, could best teach the virtues of Ashfield, Christ, adolescence, and Mansoul. Immigrants could learn American ways in the classroom. In manual training programs and in school gardens city children could be saved from dementia praecox by the kinds of skills and natural experiences that had made Ashfield such a model school for adolescence. In fact the schools might be moved entirely out of the "devil-made" city into the "God-made" country so that the cities could be completely emptied of children. Most important, the schools were the best agency for teaching the paramount civic virtue of service, "the one word now written across the zenith of the educational skies." Service was the working form of the spirit of Christ and the adolescent desire for self-sacrifice, and the teacher who taught his students to serve the "group spirit" would be a "true saint." America was in the most serious kind of danger, and the task of "civics" was supremely important. Only training for service could cut through the dense and threatening growth of urban ignorance, "hoodlumism," corrupt politics, corporate greed and industrial oppression, and the "vampires who pander to lust and debauch youth with drink . . . and prey on the virtue of young

---

[36] *Adolescence*, II, pp. 554, 558-560; *Educational Problems*, II, p. 672; *Life and Confessions*, pp. 258-353; "The Message of the Zeitgeist," *Scientific Monthly*, 13 (1921), pp. 115-116.

girls." The schools were little more to Hall than institutional in-
struments for his moral philosophy. They were his best hope that
preindustrial virtue and the needs of Mansoul might outlast and
conquer the vices and sophistication of urban, industrial capitalism.[37]

American involvement in World War I resolved any doubts
Hall may have had that his kind of morality was sorely needed
in America. He had some initial questions about the necessity for
United States participation in the fighting, but he soon committed himself to the war effort with much of Baldwin's kind of
fervor. Hall damned conscientious objectors as a "motley crew"
without a shred of the instinct for service. And, in a fit of war
fever, he decided that the ideal man was the ideal soldier, who
had "every predicate of Pauline charity and then some." Intellectually, Hall fairly welcomed the war, for it seemed to him to
prove that he had quite accurately hit upon the flaws in American
life. The country's unpreparedness, the large number of men
physically unfit to serve, the malingering of some immigrants and
intellectuals proved his basic claim that America was too rich,
too lazy, "hyper-democratic," "hyper-sophisticated," and "hyper-
individualized." The war provided a working assessment of
America and clearly tabulated the costs of the loss of moral and
physical stamina. In short, the war put a premium on the kind
of morality Hall had been teaching for thirty years. The ultimate
lesson of combat, on Hall's reading of the evidence, was that the
qualities of life in Ashfield had more survival value than the
fund of mere power at the disposal of industrialism.[38]

Like many other Americans, Hall came to regard the war as a
kind of moral purgative, an occasion to revivify American society.
In response to the challenge of war he devised a more urgent
conception of the practical debt the individual owed to Mansoul. He transformed the somewhat vague idea of "service" into

---

[37] *Educational Problems, passim,* especially I, pp. 341, 540-710; II, 178, 626,
667-682.
[38] "Some Educational Values of the War," *Pedagogical Seminary,* 25(1918),
pp. 303-307; "Morale in War and After," *Psychological Bulletin,* 15(1918),
pp. 361-426; *Morale, the Supreme Standard of Life and Conduct* (New
York, 1920), pp. 29, 41, 135, 142-143.

an exigent war ethic, "morale." Morale was an agglomerate of the ideals of physical fitness, military courage, patriotism, Christianity, and evolution. The basic principle of morale was soldierly, "always to keep ourselves, body and soul . . . at the tip-top of our condition." The war hypnotized Hall because it dramatically simplified the problems of ethics. In war, or in any other extreme crisis, ends were not so important as ordinary survival. Hall's concept of sevice had been incomplete because he was never able to propose any concrete ends toward which service should be directed. But morale had a built-in end, victory in combat. For the time being, at least, there was no need to fret about the fruits of victory. The subordination of individual to the group was a tactical necessity, and military courage was nothing but the "triumph of the instinct of social over that of individual preservation." War, in short, was an adolescent phenomenon, a forced institutionalization of the adolescent initiation into the community.[39]

Before the war Hall's concept of community was largely psychological. The bond between the individual and the race was a somewhat mysterious, instinctive, or intuitive sense of unity, largely subconscious. The war made the community's demands quite concrete and presented Hall with the occasion for proposing immediate social reforms to give the community an institutional reality. The necessity for quick reform seemed to him to be redoubled by the Russian revolution. The dangers of capitalism could no longer await a slow, evolutionary remedy, for now Bolshevism was lurking in every shadow waiting to take advantage of every shortcoming of capitalism. The threat of communism was, if anything, more dangerous than the beaten challenge of "Kaiserism," and there could be no relaxation of the war spirit. William James' proposal for a moral equivalent to war had for Hall a new urgency after the Armistice. Morale must be maintained and the war continued on the domestic front against social evils. [40]

The kinds of reforms Hall had in mind were almost purely defensive. Labor should be assured a comfortable wage because empty stomachs bred revolution. Unemployment should be kept

---

[39] *Morale*, pp. 1, 31, 140, 144.
[40] *Ibid.*, pp. 147-48.

to a minimum, because "idleness . . . fertilizes the germs of
Bolshevism." Useful organizations for workingmen ought to be
devised in order to keep them out of communist groups. Sexual
licentiousness should be controlled by arranging wages to dis-
criminate in favor of family men. The saloons ought to be kept
open to keep men from attending strike meetings. The war and
the Bolshevist scare that followed it cost Hall, for a time, his
evolutionary poise. The crisis temporarily clouded his customary
long view of the racial past and future. The situation seemed so
precarious that Hall abandoned his role as a cosmic social philosopher and came to the defense of competitive capitalism. He had,
for many years before 1917, taken a dim view of laissez-faire
economic and social policy. In the heat of war and revolution,
however, he decided that American history was a "triumphant
vindication" of competitive principles. He wanted only to soften
capitalism by easing the stress on material profits and by promoting just enough regulation to keep society from falling into
revolution.[41]

Once the immediate crisis of war and the Russian Revolution
passed, Hall regained something of his composure and revised
both his evaluation of the war and his program of reform. He
decided glumly that the war had been made by old men and
only fought by the young. While an entire generation wasted its
best lives, western civilization had entered upon an ungraceful
old age, of which the war was only the most obvious symptom.
Class hatred, Bolshevism, industrial stagnation and labor violence,
the failure of religion, individual selfishness and national greed—
these and other diseases of western civilization needed more than
a few defensive economic reforms. If Mansoul were to regain the
vigor and moral promise of youth, society would have to be
radically, though gradually, reconstructed. Instead of merely
staving off revolution, reform would have to create, over a long
run, a new social order. From the urgent, frightened measures
he advocated for the postwar crisis Hall turned to precisely the
same social program proposed by Baldwin. An unspecified kind

---

[41] *Morale,* pp. 150, 201-225. For unfavorable remarks by Hall on laissez-
faire economic and social policy, see "The Moral and Religious Training of
Children," p. 34; *Educational Problems,* I, xi. Cf. Pruett, *G. Stanley Hall,*
p. 112.

of "internationalism" must prevent a recurrence of the shabby and wasteful conflict of 1914. Then, in a long peace, a systematic scheme of eugenics could breed out the defective, criminal and insane, steadily improving the quality of Mansoul. At the same time, medicine and hygiene could prolong the useful lives of the best men in an "Indian summer" of effective wisdom. These gradual but radical reforms combined with a continuous education for service could eventually create a fundamentally different, near-perfect society.[42]

All his life, Hall insistently believed in progress. He was an evolutionist who preached love, and so he had to find a rationale for the ruthless natural elimination of the unfit. The answer, of course, was that the failure of a few to survive insured the advance of the species and the eventual development of an entire race of "supermen." Hall's psychology and ethics depended upon this basic assumption of progress. Service implied a goal, however unspecific, a conception of the future that service would help bring nearer. But the confidence had always been shadowed by doubt whether society was in fact advancing, whether the change from Ashfield to New York was evidence of progress or decline. Hall's disillusionment with the war brought the doubts to a focus, and by 1920, when he was nearly eighty, confidence and doubt existed together in his mind so closely intertwined that they were almost indistinguishable. He formulated the mingled faith and fear into a reversible vision of the future, a fantasy account of the "Fall of Atlantis."[43]

The story was reversible on almost every level. It was a utopian vision of perfection but, at the same time, a disheartening tale of disaster. To set the stage, Hall reversed time. His narrator first moved forward in time to a society sufficiently advanced in technology to discover the sunken Atlantis. Then the story moved backward in time thousands of years to describe Atlantis at its height, then forward again to describe the decline of the perfect

---

[42] *Senescence,* pp. 431-435.
[43] "Pity," pp. 590-591. Hall was fond of Nietzsche and the notion of the superman; but there was a basic difference between the two men, for Hall advocated a kind of equalitarian society in which every man would be a superman. The war, thought Hall, represented a perversion of the superman ideal simply because the Germans tried to limit the superman ideal to a country, a race, or a civilization. *Morale,* pp. 10-15.

society. The most significant reversal was that the history of the fall of Atlantis simply inverted the ordinary order of evolution. Atlantis devolved. It began as a highly organized and superbly advanced society, then slid down the evolutionary scale to the stage occupied by American society in the nineteenth and twentieth centuries. The decline continued until Atlantis devolved into barbarism and the Atlanteans began to mingle with the apes, spawning a prehistoric race of "semi-simians." Finally, Atlantis returned into the sea, the primeval source of all evolutionary life. Atlantis' decline was, in almost every detail, an evolutionary about-face for Hall. By giving his story this reversible form, Hall was able, within the same simple plot, to express his worst fears and his best hopes for Mansoul. Atlantis was both a warning and a model. The contrast between Atlantis and America in 1920 was a summation of the shortcoming of industrial capitalism, and the devolution of Atlantis was a warning. But, read in the customary evolutionary direction, the story sketched a glowing possibility of progress. It came closer than anything else Hall ever wrote to a description of an ideal society for the future, a replacement for the irrevocably lost Ashfield.[44]

Atlantis before its fall was a society of service and morale, a perfect realization of Hall's moral philosophy. The cities, the worst curse of the nineteenth century, were spotlessly hygienic, and children were taken into the country to be raised in "groves." Physical and mental disease, especially dementia praecox, were virtually unknown. Health was Atlantis' highest cult and the temple of the health-god, "Keepup," was the most splendid and popular. The schools were ideally organized around the principles of Hall's child psychology, and academicians had all the acclaim that belonged to the capitalist in Hall's America. The leading scholars went abroad "in state," had their effigies in the Atlantean "Hall of Fame," and held the highest honors the state could grant. These and a score of other consummations of Hall's desires were all products of Atlantis' syndicalist organization as a community of service. Everyone—doctors, lawyers, teachers, mothers—belonged to a guild completely devoted to the common weal. The Atlanteans redefined all the conventional economic categories of

---

44 "The Fall of Atlantis," *Recreations of a Psychologist* (New York, 1920), pp. 1-127.

capitalism. "Wealth," in Atlantis, was the ability to serve others; "enterprise" meant an extension of service; "corporation" meant, simply, cooperation. All the laws, customs, and institutions of Atlantis were elaborations of the one organic principle of the society—selfishness in any form is evil. Atlantis was, in short, a fictional model of organized adolescence, a model community in which every citizen lived not for himself but for the race.[45]

---

[45] "The Fall of Atlantis," *passim.*

Chapter 6

Josiah Royce: The Moral Community

Josiah Royce's world was a moral event. Evil was everywhere, to be challenged by good in a moral strife that reached into the farthest recesses of every man's life. Suffering, pain, injustice, sin . . . these were the inescapable conditions of existence. Job in his lament, John Bunyan in his struggles with the tempter, Lord Tennyson in the gloom of his old age, all guessed correctly at least half of the secret of creation. Only the presence of the most stubborn, genuine, unmistakable evil could give meaning to a moral universe. Even God had to suffer evil. Every human pain hurt the Absolute Being, every injustice was a divine loss, every wrong turning of man made God uneasy. But for Royce, omnipresent evil was a cause of rejoicing, because sin, pain, and death lent meaning to the human career. Every time a man denied the flesh, smote evil, and walked upright the cosmos passed minutely forward toward its goal. In the long, long run the good would triumph. Evil would not disappear from Royce's world, as it must from the world of a more mechnical optimist like Spencer, but the good would eventually get control of evil and subordinate it by strength of will.[1]

Royce was a metaphysician and spent most of his life trying to imagine the one glance with which an absolute mind might in-

---

[1] The problem of evil preoccupied Royce most of his life, but the preoccupation was most pronounced in the 1890's, when it prompted some of his best essays. See especially, "The Problem of Job," "The Case of John Bunyan," "Tennyson and Pessimism," and "The Knowledge of Good and Evil," collected in *Studies of Good and Evil: a Series of Essays upon Problems of Philosophy and of Life* (New York, 1898), pp. 1-124.

144

stantaneously perceive the moral meaning of the universe. As a matter of practice, he had to look at the world through the eyes of an ordinary man. He had to watch, somewhat impatiently, the agonizingly slow process as it spread over time. In the vision of an infinite being the world drama would require but a glimpse, but a man—even a metaphysician—had to be content with something less than perfect and immediate synopsis. For man, then, history was a particularly significant affair, because only a careful study of the progress and direction of events could provide clues to the moral direction of the world at large. History, like the cosmos, was a morality play.

Royce believed that the early history of California, his native state, was a particularly significant act in the drama. The conquest of Mexican California, the gold rush, the coming of age of San Francisco were events of such pace that they served almost as a laboratory experiment in which man was tested under conditions of maximum stress. California history was a telescoped version of the moral struggle that was basic to all history. The contest in California, Royce claimed, was a simple but deadly clash between the community and the individual irresponsibility of the settlers. The community represented moral order, the good; evil was embodied in the moral disintegration that resulted from the pioneers' individual greed. The struggle was decided, in principle, in the decade between the Mexican War and the formation of the second of San Francisco's vigilance committees in 1856.[2]

The news from Sutter's mill lured a population of social "Jonahs" to California, Royce thought, fortune hunters running from families, the law, responsibility, in search of a "fool's liberty." In the gold fields and in the towns the result was a very sordid period of social collapse, lynch law, drunkenness, gambling, mur-

---

[2] History, especially the painstaking narration of local history, is a pursuit so uncommon among metaphysicians as to be almost suspicious. Royce wrote his *California, from the Conquest in 1846 to the Second Vigilance Committee in San Francisco: a Study in the American Character* (Boston, 1886) just after he had gone east to teach at Harvard. But this by no means got California history out of his system. See also, "Montgomery and Fremont: New Documents on the Bear Flag Affair," *Century Magazine*, 41(1891), pp. 780-783; "The Fremont Legend," *Nation*, 52(1891), pp. 423-425; "An Episode of Early California Life: the Squatter Riot of 1850 in Sacramento," *Studies of Good and Evil*, pp. 298-348.

der, and mistreatment of foreigners. California was ruled by un-
checked individual avarice. But, in the 1850s, the conserving
forces of order began gradually to assert themselves. Women, the
family, churches, and schools timorously challenged the supremacy of the irresponsible individual. "In the air, as it were, the
invisible divine net of social duties hung, and, descending, en-
meshed irresistibly all the gay and careless fortune-hunters even
while they boasted of their freedom." The formation of the
second vigilance committee, in the year after Royce's birth, symbolized the triumph of order. The community at last began to be
what it ought to be, "all important as against individual doings
and interests." The lesson seemed to Royce as old as it was plain:
"It is the State, the Social Order, that is divine. We are all but
dust, save as this Social Order gives us life."[3]

The contest between the community and the private ambitions
of its members was, in Royce's eyes, the normal historical form of
the cosmic strife of good and evil. The individual was as important to Royce as to any Christian moral philosopher, but the
individual, he always believed, gained reality only by transcend-
ing the boundaries of his individuality. Alone, the individual
counted for nothing. Only as part of both a cosmic order and a
social community could the individual exist and function morally.
Royce devoted his life to trying to discover the formula of transcendence, the philosophical device by which man might be freed
of his fragmentary, insulated individuality. He explored most of
the philosophical avenues open to an intellectual of the late nineteenth century, and, along the way, he created the most elaborate and sophisticated idealism in American thought. On his
sixtieth birthday in 1915, a few months before he died, Royce
delivered an off-the-cuff summary of his philosophical career:
"When I review this whole process, I strongly feel that my deepest motives and problems have centered about the Idea of the
Community, although this idea has only gradually come to my
clear consciousness." The end result of all his metaphysical con-
structions was an assertion of the ideal of community that rivaled
and resembled Peirce's in imaginative scope and splendor.[4]

---

[3] *California*, viii, pp. 273-276, 374-376, 398, 465, 499-501.
[4] "Words of Professor Royce at the Walton Hotel at Philadelphia, December 29, 1915," *Papers in Honor of Josiah Royce on His Sixtieth Birthday*

Royce was probably the best reader that Peirce ever had. When William James looked back in the 1890s on Peirce's *Popular Science Monthly* essays of 1877 and 1878, it was the mere preliminaries, "The Fixation of Belief" and "How to Make Our Ideas Clear," that caught his vagrant eye. But Royce, reviewing Peirce's writings a decade or so after James, had a surer sense of what Peirce was driving at. It was the logical sermons on the community that compelled Royce's attention, "Some Consequences of Four Incapacities," and "Grounds of Validity of the Laws of Logic." Royce was aware of Peirce's work from the 1880s on. The two men did not correspond much until the turn of the century, but they used James as a common clearing house. They fell into a serious quarrel in the early 1890s over a severe review that Royce wrote of a book by Peirce's friend, Francis Ellingwood Abbott. After a few years, however, Peirce and Royce patched up their quarrel and became warm mutual admirers. Finally, after about 1910, Royce fell very deeply under the spell of Peirce's concept of community and spent the last years of his life adapting his own idealism to the specifications of the community of inquiry.[5]

This outcome was ironic, for Royce's career was in many ways an inversion of Peirce's. Royce was born in 1855 in Grass Valley, California, a very great cultural distance from Cambridge, Massachusetts. In 1849, while Peirce's father was expanding his intellectual reputation from within the best of America's universities, Royce's parents had loaded all their goods into a wagon and crossed the country to California. Royce's father operated a general store in the mining town of Grass Valley, and, until the family moved into San Francisco in 1866, Royce's mother conducted a small private school in the family living room. Grass Valley had no other school. Peirce learned Kant and mathematics from his father, a master in both, while Royce listened to his

(published as volume twenty-five of the *Philosophical Review,* 1916), p. 282.

[5] Royce, *Problem of Christianity* (Two volumes, New York, 1913), II, pp. 114-117; Royce and F. Kernan, "Charles Sanders Peirce," *Journal of Philosophy,* 13(1916), pp. 701-709; Royce to William James, 19 September, 1880, in Perry, *Thought and Character of William James,* I, p. 788. Peirce's very high opinion of Royce is amply apparent in his review essays on Royce's *The World and the Individual* (Two volumes, New York, 1900-1902), in Peirce, *Collected Papers,* 8.100-131.

mother reading aloud from the Bible. Almost every intellectual advantage that belonged to a Peirce in Cambridge was missing from the life of a Royce in Grass Valley or San Francisco.[6]

Royce was, by his own estimate at least, an awkward boy who had considerable difficulty getting along with his schoolmates. He had rheumatic fever in childhood and could not play the games of grammar school and high school. By the time he was ready for college, he had recovered enough to work on a college "labor crew" to help pay his way through the new University of California. Peirce more or less loafed his way to his Harvard degree, armed with all the confidence that belonged to him as a son of Benjamin Peirce. But Royce had to plot a very practical plan of life for himself. He decided to take up the distinctly Californian pursuit of mining engineering.[7]

He was a successful student, and at graduation in 1875 he was summoned to read an oration on Prometheus. His apparent command of Greek drama and mythology so impressed some of the businessmen of Berkeley and San Francisco that a group of them created a fund to finance postgraduate study in Germany. In the late summer of 1875 he set out eastward with his one suit and a letter of introduction from Daniel Coit Gilman, then president of the University of California. Royce stopped off in Boston, where he was able to arrange a very brief encounter with the most important friend of his life, William James. Peirce began life as an insider and dropped precipitately out of Harvard and Boston circles. Royce came east a poor and gawky provincial and had to spend the next decade trying to insinuate himself.[8]

Royce passed his German year in Leipsig and Gottingen. He was most attracted by the lectures of Hermann Lotze, whose neo-Kantian doctrine that the personal self is an ultimate unity was one of Royce's early postulates. Royce read Kant carefully. He

---

[6] Royce's mother wrote a memoir of the trip west, *Frontier Lady* (New Haven, 1932); Grass Valley, interestingly, is not mentioned in Royce's *California;* James Harry Cotton, *Royce on the Human Self* (Cambridge, 1954), 3; "Words of Professor Royce . . . 1915," *Papers in Honor of Josiah Royce,* pp. 279-280.

[7] Cotton, *Royce on the Human Self,* pp. 3-4; "Words of Professor Royce . . . 1915," p. 281.

[8] The University of California opened in 1873, two years before Royce obtained his degree. Cotton, *Royce on the Human Self,* p. 4; "Words of Professor Royce . . . 1915," p. 281.

also read some of Hegel, but he seldom singled Hegel out for any special attention among German philosophers. In fact he denied, from time to time, that Hegel held any particular sway over him, and he wrote as much and as often of other German philosophers like Schopenhauer, Fichte, Schelling, and Lotze. Like Hegel, Royce was a philosopher of the absolute, but the formal machinery of the dialectic was almost entirely missing from his thought. He was probably accurate in his final estimate that poets and literary theorists were as important to his German experience as any technical philosophical idealism. The artistic and moral intensity he encountered in what he called "the German Romantic school" held his attention in the early years of his career as much as any problem in philosophy. In the decade between 1875 and 1885 Royce wrote and lectured about as much on literature as on philosophy, and he even attempted a novel of his own, *Feud of Oakfield Creek*, which was a literary disaster.[9]

Royce got back to the United States in the propitious autumn when Johns Hopkins opened with Gilman in the seat of power. On a fellowship, Royce quickly completed a dissertation on "The Interdependence of Human Knowledge," and, by April of 1878, had a Ph.D. in hand and was ready for a job teaching philosophy somewhere in the east. He stayed in Baltimore for a few weeks giving public lectures on German poetry, until it became apparent that there was to be no job. He had to return to Berkeley, into what he thought of as an exile, to teach freshman composition, just a year before Peirce got his only real university opportunity at Johns Hopkins. Within a few years, the tables were completely turned. In 1885 Royce was made a regular member of the Harvard philosophy department, and two years later Peirce went into his longer and much deeper exile in Milford.

The east and Germany signified release to Royce, as New York did to Hall or Berlin to Ross. He resented having to return to what he called the "wilderness" after his tantalizing glimpses of Boston, Baltimore, Leipsig, and Gottingen. He was busy in Berkeley. His teaching took up a lot of time, and he wrote a

---

[9] "Words of Professor Royce . . . 1915," p. 282; Royce, "Schiller's Ethical Studies," *Journal of Speculative Philosophy* (1878), and "Shelly and the Revolution," *The Californian* (1880), both reprinted in *Fugitive Essays by Josiah Royce*, J. Loewenberg, ed. (Cambridge, 1920), pp. 41-95; *Feud of Oakfield Creek, a Novel of California Life* (Boston, 1887).

Primer of Logical Analysis for his English students and several articles for western journals, *The Overland Monthly* and *The Californian*. He also published two essays in the *Journal of Speculative Philosophy* and two very ambitious pieces in the prestigious English journal, *Mind*.[10] He was, as he put it, "among friends" and he got married. But despite all the activity, he felt restless and isolated.

> There is no philosophy in California [he wrote to James]—from Siskiyou to Ft. Yuma, from the Golden Gate to the summit of the Sierras. . . . I trumped up a theory of logical concepts last term and preached it to the seniors. . . . It was monstrous, and, in this wilderness with nobody to talk with about it, I have not the least idea whether it is true or not.[11]

James' response to Royce's complaints about California were usually mixtures of bad jokes and good promises, promises that James kept when he went on leave in 1882 and arranged for Royce to replace him. But James also gave Royce a striking clue to the situation of the intellectual even in Cambridge. "You are not so very much isolated in California. We are all isolated— 'columns left alone of a temple once complete.'" It was a warning that Royce might well have taken to heart, for after he had gained academic security at Harvard he never felt quite at home, and his memory reverted very often to California. In the 1880s and 1890s he wrote California history, and after the turn of the century he began to advocate "provincialism" as a counter to the impersonal alienations of American life:

> There is a rather large proportion of people who either have not grown up where they were born, or who have changed their dwelling-place in adult years. . . . I myself, as a native of California, now resident in New England, belong to such a class. Such classes, even in modern New England, are too large.

In the end Royce was almost as nostalgically attached to California as Ross was to Iowa or Hall to Ashfield. California represented a potential identity with a concretely existing community,

---

[10] *Primer of Logical Analysis for the Use of Composition Students* (San Francisco, 1881); most of the essays of the California period have been reprinted in *Fugitive Essays*.
[11] Royce to William James, January 14, 1879, in Perry, *Thought and Character of William James*, I, p. 781.

and toward California Royce felt "native," whereas toward New England he only felt "resident."[12]

In the midst of his Berkeley exile, even while he was writing his complaints to James, Royce felt inevitably rooted in California. "I am a Californian," he wrote in a prefatory note for a proposed book, "and day after day . . . I am accustomed to be found at my tasks at a certain place that looks down upon the Bay of San Francisco." It was, to be sure, unpleasant to be "preaching in this wilderness." But the wilderness was at least his and the place, as he put it, "certain." That much was so, he thought wryly, "by order of the World Spirit (whose commands we all do ever obey, whether we will it or no)." In a sense the problem of life for Royce was that when he left California, he lost a sense of direct contact with the "World Spirit" and had to construct and reconstruct a succession of merely metaphysical absolutes. The motive for the presence of the absolute in Royce's philosophy was to unite men's personal selves in a supra-personal unity. But Royce was always looking, restlessly, for present, concrete, working manifestations of the unity, and one of his best hopes for an actual community on earth was the "province," the very California from which he tried so hard in the 1870s and 1880s to escape. He was less a geographical itinerant than most American intellectuals of the period, certainly less so than Peirce, Baldwin, Ross, or Hall. But the result of his one long move was the same kind of dissatisfaction with the private person and a quest for a philosophical theory that could promise membership in an ultimately satisfying community.[13]

The fragmentary self was one of the key problems of Royce's philosophy. He was constantly making revisions in his idealism, but his analysis of the self remained quite constant throughout his career from the publication in 1885 of his first major work, *The Religious Aspect of Philosophy*, through *The World and the*

---

[12] James to Royce, February 3, 1880, in Perry, *Thought and Character of William James*, I, p. 787; Royce, "Provincialism," a lecture of 1902, in *Race Questions, Provincialism and Other American Problems* (New York, 1908), pp. 68-69.

[13] A diary entry, dated February 12, 1879, in *Fugitive Essays*, pp. 6-7.

Individual in 1900-1902, to *The Problem of Christianity* in 1913. Royce, like every other major American thinker of the period, participated in the thorough destruction of the notion of an innate self or soul. He denied the existence of any "Soul-Substance" which was given to rather than gotten from experience, whether the experience was evolutionary, social, or personal. What passed for a self, from Descartes through Kant, was actually only "a mere collection of accidental experiences and processes . . . a mere heap of feelings, of associations, of beliefs." The problem of philosophy was to discover how this "heap" of fleeting moments became organized into a personality. Man's endowment was only "a cauldron of seething and bubbling efforts to be somebody."[14]

"Becoming somebody" always meant to Royce getting a purpose. Both the self and the world the self experienced were the products of active, willing purpose. Ideas, he agreed with James and Dewey, were "plans of action," which men willed to believe. Only a purpose, a "life-plan" could transform the "heap" of fragmentary moments of awareness into an organized personality and, in the process, will into existence the organized world of experience. "In each moment," Royce wrote to James as early as 1880, "we construct a world because we are interested in doing so. . . . 'Give me a world' is the cry of consciousness; and behold, a world is made even in the act of crying." Without willing purpose there was no self, only a succession of discrete cognitive moments. But, given a purpose, the past and future could be, as Royce put it, "postulated" and organized into a meaningful system of memories and hopes that constituted a personality. "*By this meaning of my life-plan . . . I am defined and created a self.*"[15]

This analysis of the purposive nature of the self, which Royce repeated in varying guises for thirty years, did not really solve any problem. It only made the problem more specific. It enabled Royce to translate the question, "how does the self arise," into the more practical question, "how does purpose become a part

---

14 *The Conception of God* (2 ed., New York, 1897), pp. 276-277; *The Philosophy of Loyalty* (New York, 1908), p. 172.
15 *Outlines of Psychology: an Elementary Treatise with Some Practical Applications* (New York, 1903), 288-292. "How Beliefs are Made," *The Californian* (1882), in *Fugitive Essays,* 343-363; Royce to William James, September 19, 1880, in Perry, *Thought and Character of William James,* I, 276.

of consciousness." The question was thorny. To merely have asserted that the will was an innate "principle" would have been a reversion to the concept of the original self which Royce, in company with his contemporaries, was trying to avoid. Neither the organized will nor the organized self could be original, and neither could precede the other. What Royce required was an account of the simultaneous genesis of the will and the self. He found the basic solution in Baldwin's dialectic of personal growth.

Royce pounced on Baldwin's analysis of the origin of the self almost as soon as Baldwin announced it in *Mental Development in the Child and the Race.* The concept of the self as, mainly, the product of imitation of other selves solved the problem of the common origin of will and self. The child by imitating other people (projects, as Baldwin called them), learned, in effect, to copy their will. In the act of imitation the child experienced willing behavior and, as Baldwin concluded, eventually exerted a will of his own on other, weaker persons, Baldwin's ejects. The result of the dialectical process of imitation and aggression was the formation of a will, of what Baldwin called an "ideal self," or, in Royce's terminology, a "life-plan." The life-plan for Royce was virtually the self. It molded the diffuse and diverse collection of impulses and sensations into a self-conscious, purposeful, individual personality. For Royce, as much as for Peirce, Baldwin, Hall, or Ross, the self was thoroughly social. "I am dependent on my fellows, not only physically, but to the very core of my conscious self-hood, not only for what, physically speaking, I am, but for what I take myself to be." Royce pressed the consequences of the dialectic of personal growth further than Baldwin, Royce claimed that men's ideas of the external, physical world were also social in origin. In order to conceive his own self a man first had to conceive other selves, but, in turn, he also had to insist on the reality of the other selves' experiences. To do this he must postulate, at least provisionally, the reality of the physical world the other selves claimed to experience. In such ways every idea, every plan of action depended on the membership of men in societies of other men.[16]

---

[16] "Self-Consciousness, Social Consciousness, and Nature," an address of 1895, in *Studies of Good and Evil,* p. 201. For Royce's uses of Baldwin, see *Outlines of Psychology,* pp. 274-298; *World and the Individual,* II, pp. 256-265; *Philosophy of Loyalty,* pp. 24-38, and most especially "Some Ob-

Baldwin's purpose was only to give a theoretical account of
the substantial harmony between individuals and their societies,
and Royce was satisfied with this much of Baldwin's effort. But
the genetic analysis of the self, like any evolutionary historicism,
carried a heavy burden of ethical relativism. Within any genetic
framework there could be no absolute conception of the good.
Every culture justified the kinds of moral individuals it produced.
The fundamental presupposition of every genetic theory, whether
biological, psychological, or historical, is that the nature of anything is explained by its past development. But the obvious conclusion to be drawn from this presupposition (drawn by a Veblen,
for example, or a Sumner) is that genesis not only explains but
makes valid its results. This was the kind of consequence that
Royce wanted desperately to avoid. He was led, during the years
from about 1885 to about 1910, into a backhanded war on science
to escape the relativist conclusions of evolution.[17]

Royce believed, during these years, that ethics and science had
to have radically different premises. Science was possible only on
the unfounded assumption that the universe was absolutely
regular. The methods of science involved, first, abstraction and
then explanation. To be able to report, as opposed to "appreciate,"
a phenomenon, a man first had to abstract, to describe the phenomenon as just one of a type or class. Then, to explain the
phenomenon, the scientific man had to assert that phenomena of
one type were always followed or accompanied by phenomena of
another type. Science, in other words, could only inquire into a
cosmos that it presumed to be deterministic in the strongest possible sense, a mechanical cosmos whose every subsequent state
was latent in the original "star-mist." In such a universe no al-
lowance could be made for chance or real novelty.[18]

servations on the Anomalies of Self-Consciousness," an address of 1894 to
the Medico-Psychological Association of Boston, in *Studies of Good and
Evil*, pp. 169-197. The argument for the social sources of conceptions of
nature is put most fully in *World and the Individual*, II, pp. 165-180.
[17] For Royce's horror of moral indeterminacy, see "Pessimism and Modern
Thought," *Berkeley Quarterly* (1880), in *Fugitive Essays*, pp. 176-182.
[18] Royce's argument on ethics and science is most strenuously made in
"Natural Law, Ethics and Evolution," one of a series of papers by various
authors on Huxley's Romanes lectures, in *International Journal of Ethics*
(1895), in *Studies of Good and Evil*, pp. 125-139. The same position is
stated in more gentle form in *World and the Individual*, II, pp. 180-204.
See also *The Spirit of Modern Philosophy* (Boston, 1892), pp. 294-300, 363-
368, 415-434.

Ethics, in sharp contrast, was precisely a matter of novelty and chance. Desire, to Royce, implied uncertainty. If a scientific man believed thoroughly and sincerely in his deterministic assumptions, he could desire nothing, have no ideals. The perfect scientist would be incapable of any willing, ethical behavior. Every explanation of a natural fact offered by science, if it were accepted as a true explanation of a real fact, narrowed the scope of ethics. And if science could offer an explanation of so much as one fact, science could, in principle, explain every fact. There could, then, be no such thing as a real desire, and ethics would be an illusion.[19]

The model of "science" Royce had in mind was, of course, Herbert Spencer, and like most every American intellectual, Royce rejected most of the Spencerian attitude out of hand. Indeed the American following of Spencer was an illusion that existed mainly in the minds of Spencer himself and publicists like Henry Holt and Edward Livingston Youmans. Spencer had scores of American readers, for a brief course in Spencer was a prerequisite to education for any American who matured after 1860. But the American uses of Spencer were confined almost entirely to accepting only the bits and pieces of the system that could be used to advantage against the main structure. Spencer may have had a kind of following in something that could be called a "reading public." But among intellectuals of real stature—Peirce, Oliver Wendell Holmes, William James, Hall, Baldwin, Ward, Ross, George Herbert Mead, Charles H. Cooley, Dewey, Veblen, and so on down a list that would virtually exhaust the *dramatis personae* of the period—Spencer was more whipping boy than master.

Royce was a daring and skillful whipper. His technique of attacking Spencer or any other scientific positivist was simply to deny that science described the real universe. The assumptions of science, its abstractions and explanations, were useful conventions which, for the moment, seemed to help men go about their business. In the last resort, however, the deterministic universe of science was not real. The real universe was a universe

---

[19] Royce almost never attacked Spencer frontally and by name, but it is perfectly plain that Spencer was the model of science that he had in mind. For some early strictures on the Spencerian point of view, see "The Nature of Voluntary Progress," *Berkeley Quarterly* (1879), in *Fugitive Essays*, pp. 96-97, 104-105, 110-111.

of novelty, growth, of a genuine evolution whose path was not already fixed in the star-mist. By denying Spencer's universe the status of a reality, Royce could also escape the ragged dualism of Huxley's Romanes lecture of 1893, in which Huxley made his famous claim that there were two radically different but equally real processes, "cosmical" and "ethical." Royce's analysis of the assumptions of science forced the conclusion that if there was a cosmical process at all, then there could not possibly be a co-existent ethical process. He opted for the ethical process, for a world in which "at every instant of time . . . something novel, significant, individual, and in its own measure free, occurs, and leads to new results for which the choices of finite moral agents are responsible."[20]

Royce was an intellectual in search of assurances, but his denial of the scientific orderliness of nature and the presence in his philosophical world of novelty created a potentially disastrous lack of assurances. This was one of Royce's key technical problems—the construction of a world view that allowed freedom and chance without degenerating into chaotic disorder. One of the most essential roles played by the idea of the absolute in Royce's system was the reconciliation of freedom and order. The absolute served other needs to be sure. Royce believed only an absolute purpose could make individual purposes possible; only an absolute experience could make individual experiences possible; only an absolute thought could make individual thoughts possible; and only an absolute truth could make individual errors possible. But, in addition to performing these manifold and important intellectual tasks, the concept of the absolute enabled Royce to deny the "cosmical process" without lapsing into a despairing philosophy of utter indeterminacy.[21]

---

[20] "Natural Law, Ethics and Evolution," pp. 136-139; *World and the Individual*, II, p. 369.

[21] The absolute appears, directly or by implication, on almost every page of Royce's works published through 1908. See especially the famous chapter on "The Possibility of Error," in *The Religious Aspect of Philosophy* (Boston, 1885); "The Implications of Self-Consciousness," *New World* (1892), in *Studies of Good and Evil*, pp. 140-168; *The Spirit of Modern Philosophy* (Boston, 1892), pp. 372-380, 454-471; *World and the Individual*, I, pp. 40-42, 345-384, II, pp. 418-420. A superb exposition of Royce's absolute idealism is Gabriel Marcel, *Royce's Metaphysics* trans. by Virginia and Gordon Ringer (Chicago, 1956). Marcel's lucid study was originally published in 1918-1919 in France, where Royce got considerable attention.

In the construction of the absolute, a task that occupied him from about 1885 to about 1910, Royce turned the Spencerian world inside out. Spencer claimed that a physical world, passing from one state to another according to strict laws of succession, was the primary reality. Within this world there was room for only an unverifiable supposition that there might be a universal purpose, which Spencer condescendingly included among the things unknowable. For Royce the universal, absolute purpose was the primary reality. Within the world created by this purpose there was room for only an unverifiable supposition that the physical world was law-abiding. Royce's world was as orderly as Spencer's. The difference was that Spencer's order was inherent in the natural process itself, whereas Royce's order was the expression of the moral purpose, the "rational will" of the absolute.

Basically, the absolute was an infinite consciousness or thought. It was aware of the whole universe during the entire time-span, but the awareness took the form of one thought. As Royce liked to say, the absolute viewed the work all at a glance, *totum simul.* But the absolute was not a mere knower, for it also was absolute will or purpose. In the finite, fragmentary experiences of individual men, purposes were thwarted, wills unfulfilled. In the absolute, willing and experiencing were simultaneous. The absolute experience was perfectly identical with the absolute will, and the universe was the immediate satisfaction of infinite purpose. Therefore, Royce could conclude, the universe could be both a novelty and an order. The freedom and chance men experienced were real, but in the synoptic experience of the absolute there was no chance because there was no temporal separation of the will and the satisfaction.

This reconciliation of order and freedom was only Royce's method of performing the ubiquitous intellectual task given to his generation—working out a substitute for the inherited view of man as a self-sufficient individual. The task was just as important a motive for Royce as it was for Peirce, Baldwin, Ross, or Hall. His conception of the task and his technical performance of it were different. The basic difficulty he was trying to solve was the same. He was as convinced as any of his contemporaries that the individual, alone, was a moral cipher, incapable of real experience let alone good conduct. Before about 1910, Royce believed that the concept of the absolute formally solved the problem of individuality. The enormous flexibility of the idea of a universal self enabled him, simultaneously, to assert and deny the individuality of the human self. The absolute was "many" because it included the great host of real individuals, each with a will of his own, but in the absolute each private man gained ultimate publicity and total unity with all other men as one finite consummation of absolute purpose. Royce defined individuality, voluntaristically, as "just my conscious intent to be, in God's world, myself and nobody else." He was confident this individual act of will was identical with the absolute will. So there was no contradiction, in the last resort, between individuality and universality.[22]

Royce spent about thirty years elaborating his absolute idealism, and the result was technically imposing (even to William James) and formally symmetrical. But the very formality of the system was its great shortcoming. The absolute satisfied only half of Royce's mind. It provided him with a coherent and attractive world view, but the absolute did not offer any ready answers to practical questions about what Royce or any other man ought to do about concrete, American problems. William James, in his long and intimate philosophical contest with Royce, usually concentrated on the maddening respose of the absolute. Royce, as James said, always assured his readers that all was well with the absolute, "Him," but the self-assurance of the absolute only invited its worshippers to take what James cunningly called a "moral holiday." As James well knew, Royce wanted anything but a moral holiday. Royce constantly reiterated his belief in the real presence of evil in the world and in the obligation of men to

---

[22] The logical reconciliation of the oneness and manyness of the absolute was the technical problem Royce dealt with in the "Supplementary Essay" to *World and the Individual*, I. pp. 473-598. See *Ibid.*, II, pp. 326-331, 434-437; *The Conception of God* (Second ed., New York, 1897), pp. 291-293, 302, 350-351; *The Sources of Religious Insight* (New York, 1912), pp. 160-161. *The Sources of Religious Insight* was the first of Royce's books (leaving aside the history of California) in which "Absolute" did not begin the index. By 1912 Royce's interest in the absolute had been almost completely supplanted by an interest in community. On this change, see Peter Fuss, *The Moral Philosophy of Josiah Royce* (Cambridge, 1965), pp. 259-263.

engage in an unrelenting, strenuous contest with every form of evil. By the turn of the century the formal deduction of the absolute from the facts of experience was complete. Royce announced it in a stunning technical performance in the Gifford lectures at Aberdeen in 1899 and 1900. But the technical deduction completed only half the task, the other half was to give concreteness to the working relationship that man in his affairs ought to have with the absolute. Royce spent the remainder of his career on this more difficult task. The final result was that he abandoned the formal absolute in favor of the kind of concept of community he rediscovered in Peirce. He gave up the quest for the absolute to join in the quest for community.[23]

From the point of view of the absolute, if the absolute had anything as concrete as a *point* of view, the relationship between the one and the many was clear enough. The absolute encompassed and defined all of its member-selves. From the angle of vision of the ordinary, morally embattled man, however, the relationship was unhappily vague. Satisfaction with the formal status of being "included" within the absolute might, in fact, promote the kind of moral holiday that James had accused Royce of fostering. What Royce had to do was to spell out the concrete steps a man ought to take to put himself into a willing, working relationship to the infinite self. Royce's ethical device was "loyalty," a formula he developed in 1906-1908 lectures to teachers and divinity students at Harvard, Yale, and other universities in the east and midwest. Royce must have felt that the teachers and future ministers who would conduct the wars of the Lord in America needed some ethical counsel more practical than the formal assurances he had made available in his technical books. He hoped to demonstrate, in the *Philosophy of Loyalty*, that

> such philosophical idealism as I have long maintained is not a doctrine remote from life, but is in close touch with the most practical issues. . . . I am writing . . . for all those who love their country,—a country so ripe at present for idealism and so confused, nevertheless, by the vastness of the complication of its social and political problems.

In his preliminary definition Royce painstakingly emphasized the

---

[23] James, *Essays in Pragmatism*, Alburey Castell, ed. (New York, 1948), pp. 153-154. Cf. Royce, *Philosophy of Loyalty*, pp. 395-396; *Sources of Religious Insight*, p. 207.

strongly practical quality of loyalty, *"the willing and practical and thoroughgoing devotion of a person to a cause."*[24]

The most primitive value of loyalty was that it reconciled the two sides of the "bipolar self" that Royce took over from Baldwin. There was the private self of habit and the social self of accommodation, and they were in unresolved psychological tension. The primary need of life was to unify the social and private halves of the self so that conduct would be harmonious. But the unification could not sacrifice either side of the bipolar self. The individual must not become either a mere social automaton or an aggressor against society. Loyalty, Royce thought, created the desired unity. Loyalty to a cause gave life to the social self by uniting it with other men who served the same cause. The cause also satisfied the demands of the egoistic self of habit because the individual chose his own cause and served it with his own will. Any ontological considerations aside, loyalty was a practical good to the individuals who practiced it.[25]

Loyalties created working collectives—families, labor unions, armies, nations—in which individuals could simultaneously save and sacrifice their individuality. A cause, as a concrete ethical fact, served much the same function for Royce as the absolute did in his metaphysics. Causes unified individuals into operating communities, but the servants of the cause still retained their integrity by virtue of their own voluntary decision to serve the cause. The difficulty with causes (a difficulty they did not share with the much neater absolute) was that there were in the world conflicting causes that threatened to devour each other. "If loyalty is a supreme good, the mutually destructive conflict of loyalties is in general a supreme evil."[26]

The multiplicity and potential antagonism of the various causes available to men were only instances of Royce's perennial prob-

[24] *Philosophy of Loyalty,* v, ix, xi, p. 17; *Sources of Religious Insight,* pp. 165-167.
[25] *Philosophy of Loyalty,* pp. 16-48; "Some Relations of Physical Training to the Present Problems of Moral Education in America," an address of 1907 to the Physical Education Association of Boston, in *Race Questions, Provincialism and Other American Problems* (New York, 1908), pp. 232-242; *Sources of Religious Insight,* pp. 197-201.
[26] *Philosophy of Loyalty,* pp. 107-116; "Some Relations of Physical Training to the Present Problems of Moral Education," *Race Questions,* pp. 242-243; *Sources of Religious Insight,* p. 202.

lem, moral relativism. The psychological satisfaction that any individual might derive from service to his particular cause was not a satisfactory grounding for ethics. There had to be a formula for choosing among conflicting loyalties, an ethical imperative worthy of the absolute. Royce's answer was simple: "a cause is good, not only for me, but for mankind, in so far as it is essentially *a loyalty to loyalty*, that is, as an aid and a furtherance of loyalty in my fellows." Loyalty itself was the great cause, capable of uniting all mankind into one community of service. There would always be specific causes aimed at specific ends, but if these causes also helped to increase the total fund of loyalty in the human community, there were integral parts of the grand cause of mankind at large. Between any two causes that both furthered the cause of loyalty itself, there could, of course, be no real antagonism.[27]

The categorical imperative, "Be loyal to loyalty," fitted neatly into Royce's absolute idealism. The absolute, he thought, was still necessary to make possible any ultimate decision as to which causes did, in truth, contribute to loyalty at large. But the philosophy of loyalty had an urgency and immediacy about it that had been missing from Royce's earlier books, a concern with the American situation, with the apparent disintegration of values in the late nineteenth century. Loyalty was, in fact, a conservative ethical ideal. Royce was disturbed by the "dangerous opponents of our moral traditions," the "modern revolt against moral traditions," the "restless spirit of our reforming age."

> For what is science worth, and what is religion worth, if human life itself, for whose ennoblement science and religion have both labored, has no genuine moral standards by which one may measure its value. If, then, our moral standards themselves are questioned, the iron of doubt—so some of us feel—seems to enter our very hearts.

Behind the intricate metaphysics of Royce's idealism lay his conservative attachment to what he liked to call "our conventional morality." Philosophy, of course, was a critical discipline, and life itself ought to be a process of revision. But there were certain moral principles that Royce did not think should be subjected to serious challenge. When the "restlessness" of a Marx, a Henry George, a

---

[27] *Philosophy of Loyalty*, pp. 116-146; *Sources of Religious Insight*, pp. 202-210.

Tolstoi, or a Nietzsche threatened even the sanctity of private property and the family, Royce was ready to call a halt.[28]

Royce's affection for Baldwin involved, then, more than an intellectual agreement on questions of psychology. Both men were frightened by the prospect of moral erosion, and they both were straining to find new expressions for the old morality. Baldwin's formula was a genetic psychology with some idealistic consequences. Royce was an idealist who bent genetic psychology to his own uses. The difference was one of emphasis and training, but the purpose was the same for both men—the preservation of the same basic ethical precepts and social arrangements. Royce and Baldwin were by no means the innocent captives of moral optimism and certitude. They were as aware of the presence of evil in the world as any of the "reckless" questioners of whom they were so frightened; however, their response to evil was not to foment moral revolution but to urge more strenuous moral effort within the inherited framework.

The philosophy of loyalty was not a new ethical precept designed to replace an outworn code. Loyalty merely gathered the older conceptions of "conscience" into a neater bundle. Loyalty preserved intact all the homely virtues of benevolence, justice, honesty, patriotism, even courtesy. Royce thought that the "good old word," loyalty, systematized these virtues, organized conscience into something more than a collection of "dictates." Loyalty also made conscience intellectually respectable by showing that conscientious loyalty was a principle derived from the most modern findings of evolutionary social psychology. But for all its glistening modernity the philosophy of loyalty still buttressed the existing popular notions of right and wrong and the existing social arrangements. In fact loyalty, like Baldwin's ideal self, was quite carefully crafted to salvage conventional social and ethical attitudes.[29]

Almost by definition, for example, loyalty was well suited to restore the family. Royce thought that the disintegration of the centralized, patriarchal, well-ordered family was one of the most fearful characteristics of modern American life. Whatever else

---

[28] *Philosophy of Loyalty,* pp. 3-6; "On Certain Limitations of the Thoughtful Public in America," an address of c. 1905 at Vassar College, in *Race Questions,* pp. 160-165.
[29] *Philosophy of Loyalty,* pp. 149-153, 172-184.

loyalty might accomplish, it could at least preserve the stable family life that had sustained earlier generations of Americans. Royce also hoped that loyalty would weave a conserving net of social harmony to quell the dangerous strife between rich and poor, labor and the corporations. Royce, like Baldwin, was vaguely aware of what he called "corporate misdeeds." Like Baldwin, he feared "ill-advised labor agitations" much more. His emphasis, like that of most conservators, was on social harmony, which could result only from a loyal renunciation by all hands of selfish class ends.[30]

Most important, Royce believed, was the power of the principle of loyalty to preserve the rights of private property and other "formal obligations" and "definable relations" among men. It was such private rights and obligations that he had in mind when he expressed confidence that the principle of loyalty would "leave the liberties of the people intact." Respect for private property seemed to him to be inherent in the very notion of loyalty. If one man wantonly took another's property, he deprived his victim of the very means of expressing loyalty to any cause, so any "aggression" against private property was a "crime against humanity at large." Royce's political and economic ideas always remained essentially those of the Berkeley and San Francisco businessmen who had financed his year in Germany. His critique of individualism was psychological and metaphysical, not economic or political. In the main, he was simply frightened by turn-of-the-century America, and fright provoked the usual conservative response, a reassertion of what he thought were traditional concepts of property and obligation.[31]

Royce was most frightened by what he called, in Hegelian language, the "self-estranged social mind." A social mind that was not "estranged" was one in which individuals thought of their social unity in familiar, "homelike" terms. The social mind of a small, integrated community like San Francisco in 1856 (or Hall's Ashfield or Ross's natural community of Iowa) was at one with itself. In an "imperial" society, such as the Roman Empire, France under Louis XIV, or, sadly, the modern United States, there was a grave psychological gulf between the citizen

---

[30] *Philosophy of Loyalty*, pp. 221-223, 227-228, 230-231.
[31] *Ibid.*, pp. 159, 204, 211.

and the society at large. The alienated individual could no longer view society and the state as extensions of himself, bearing the familiar features of his own personality and conscious of him as a member. Society became abstracted, and government took on the aspect of an alien force of nature. The attitude of the citizen was one of grudging submission to a superior and foreign power. The self-estranged society was a perversion of the kind of loyal community Royce wanted to help create, and America, even more than Europe, was beginning to be guilty of the perversion.[32]

The causes and the symptoms of self-estrangement were as obvious to Royce as they were deplorable. The rush of immigration made it more and more difficult to maintain the core of moral homogeneity. The material prosperity created by industrialism caused men to labor for their own selfish success and not loyally on behalf of a cause. The collapse of the family and the extreme geographical mobility of the Americans turned society into a woefully unstable mass of isolated individuals. The nation was simply too big to attract the loyalties of its citizens, except in time of crisis, and so in practice there festered numerous psuedo-loyalties to labor unions, corporations, political parties, religious sects. These pseudo-causes had a very dangerous effect on their servants. The political hack, the union member, the employee of the corporation, usually cut off from family and birthplace, lost all individuality. Regimentation in the pseudo-cause repressed individual variety and, as a result, created the "greatest danger of popular government," the "mob-spirit." Like Baldwin, Royce thought that the aimless, lurching crowd was the end product of the whole combination of American ills, urbanization, standardization, ease of communication, and the epidemic rootlessness of the people.[33]

Against these growing perversions of loyalty and community, Royce was "not planning any social reform which would wholly do away with these conditions." He was much too conservative to tamper with the basic structure of society. He proposed only

---

[32] *Philosophy of Loyalty*, pp. 238-242.
[33] *Ibid.*, pp. 211-212, 219-223, 227-232; "Provincialism," an address at Iowa State University in 1902, in *Race Questions*, pp. 68-69.

the subdivision of national life by an ironic return to the provincialism he had so deplored during his California exile. The self-estrangement of the social mind might be cured by a revival of local loyalties. Provincial museums, the beautification of provincial capitals, the preservation of local history, and the celebration of regional folklore, all ought to be pursued in the provincial program. The kinds of stability Ross hoped to protect in Iowa and Hall in Ashfield, Royce wanted to see recreated in a variety of provinces. He named only two, significantly, the Pacific Coast and New England, and he had no extensive programmatic proposals to make. In fact he seemed to know that he was grasping at straws; however, the national malaise demanded solutions, even from a man who was more comfortable with the absolute than with problems of labor and immigration. The province was his only concrete antidote to domestic crisis. A wise provincialism would not challenge other provincial loyalties or attempt to detract from the loyalties due to the nation, of course, but the provinces might provide a series of centripetal counters to the whirling disintegration that threatened the social fabric.[34]

The ideal of the absolute was always distressingly remote in Royce's thought. In the philosophy of loyalty and its integral provincialism the absolute became not only remote but vestigial. Loyalty was an individual good, and loyalty to loyalty was an absolute law only in the sense of being categorical. The absolute was not nearly so necessary to Royce's work on loyalty as it had been to his earlier philosophy, and the province had only the barest connection with an infinite self of all selves. As the absolute dwindled, Royce's emphasis on working forms of human community grew. In the end the absolute practically disappeared from his thought and was replaced by the community. As an idea, the community behaved in much the same way the absolute did, but the change from one to the other was not a mere change in words, for it had consequences that would not have followed from a mere shift in usage. The most important difference was that the community could be approached, whereas the absolute

---

[34] *Philosophy of Loyalty*, pp. 243-248; "Provincialism," *Race Questions*, pp. 100-108; "The Pacific Coast," an address to the National Geographical Society, 1898, in *Ibid.*, pp. 201-225.

resisted all of Royce's efforts to bring it within striking distance. The community was actually present whenever as few as three men gathered together in the proper spirit. The community did not merely encompass the universe and know it *totum simul*. It was a contingent product of human efforts, existing entirely in time, struggling to grow without any ultimate assurance it would ever complete itself.[35]

Royce cast the exposition of the concept of community in the form of a solution to the "problem of Christianity." The choice was congenial, for he had always been a religious philosopher. He had no formal creed and was often harshly critical of institutional religions. The absolute bore little resemblance to any familiar concept of God, but Royce was still at home within the conventions and categories of Christianity. His illustrations of philosophical problems were chosen, as often as not, from scripture or religious history. His style was biblical and pastoral. The language of "salvation," "guilt," "disciple," "preaching in the wilderness" was, in fact, more congenial to him than the other nineteenth-century vocabulary of "adaptation," "survival," "process," or "force." Unlike Baldwin or Hall, Royce never seriously considered the ministry as a vocation, but he still conceived his role in much the same way.

Royce reinterpreted in social terms what he thought were the three fundamental articles of Christianity—original sin, atonement, and the community. He claimed that he was only explicating the Pauline statement of the faith, but he actually reviewed Christianity with the tools of social philosophy—his own, Baldwin's and Peirce's. His analysis of the nature of sin was, in outline, derived from Baldwin's conception of the self. Royce's notion of atonement was largely a reworking of his own philosophy of loyalty, and his doctrine of what the community ought to be was an adaptation of Peirce's essays of the 1860s and 1870s. Sin, he claimed, was simply a product of the transaction between society and the individual. Society set models for the individual to follow, but in the very act of bending the individual to the collective will society created the individual's own self-will. Social training bred respect for the law into citizens. Simul-

---

[35] *The Problem of Christianity* (Two volumes, New York, 1913), II, pp. 35-49.

taneously, however, this training made the individual conscious
of what Paul called the "other law" in "his members" or what
Baldwin called the egoistic self of habit and aggression. The
resulting inner division of the self, the "disease of self-consciousness" was precisely what Christianity had always called sin. The
sin was original because it resulted from man's unavoidably social
nature.[36]

Against sin, Christianity preached atonement. Historically, a
variety of different sects and theologians had meant different
things by redemption. To Royce atonement meant simply loyalty.
The individual could find salvation only by "thoroughgoing and
loving devotion . . . to a community," and Royce believed that
this was what Paul had intended to be the antidote for sin. Community was the central doctrine of a correct Christianity. Es-
trangement from the community was sin, and atonement was
recovery of membership in the community. Not only Christianity
but also all philosophy, even the moral life itself, depended upon
the existence of a true community.[37]

Such stress on an ideal community made it mandatory for
Royce to do something Peirce had never explicitly done, to make
a distinction between such societies as actually existed on earth
and true community. A society was only an accidental, historical
collective, even if it were as large as the human race itself. Institutions, language, history, symbols were not sufficient to create
a genuine community. Even the historical church, which made
the most systematic claims to representing the blessed community
on earth, had fallen far short. The social collective actually created sin by creating the divided self. Only community could cure
the division, make man psychologically whole.[38]

The problem of community was, to Royce, technically a problem of knowledge. According to classical notions of knowledge,
cognition was perception, conception, or a compounding of the
two. But, however percept and concept were arranged, they
could never yield knowledge of other minds, real communication.
Within the limitations of perception and conception men could
never escape the dualism of self and other and were doomed to be

[36] *Problem of Christianity*, I, pp. 140-147, 176-179.
[37] *Ibid.*, I, xxxvii, pp. 185-205.
[38] *Ibid.*, I, pp. 405-406.

individuals. Societies composed of such individuals were just as doomed to be mere collectives, convenient arrangements for the conduct of life, but far from the kinds of communities that could save man from the burden of his insulated finitude and his divided soul. Only genuine communication could create a saving community.

Royce attacked the puzzle of communication with a theory of "interpretation," taken largely from Peirce's theory of knowledge and doctrine of signs. Royce translated Peirce to mean that conscious experience was a process in which one thought interpreted another thought to a third thought. The third thought then became an object of interpretation by another to yet another. Here, Royce claimed, was a form of knowledge that was neither percept nor concept nor any combination of the two. Interpretation, a third and most important manner of cognition, was the basis of self-knowledge, which was only an interpretation of a past self by a present self to a future self. Any three men might form a community of interpretation clearly and radically distinct from a collective. A community of interpretation required three "neighbors" willing to engage in the activity loyally. In a successful interpretation among men the knowledge that had previously been granted only to the absolute in Royce's thought was brought to earth, for the successful act of interpretation among men required a kind of supra-personal knowledge that no single man could have. It was necessary "for my interpretation of you to our neighbor to be such as you would accept and also such as our neighbor would comprehend, were each of us already in the position of the ideal observor from above." The desire to interpret correctly was, Royce claimed, only the spirit of loyalty in more technical guise.[39]

This modification of Peirce enabled Royce to reconcile himself with science at last, for now he could look on science not as a mere set of reprehensible assumptions about the world but as a progressive activity of men loyally perfecting the interpretive method. The antagonism between science and morality or religion melted away, and Royce, like Peirce, could "look forward to a time when the work and the insight of religion can become as progressive as is now the work of science." The church had

---

[39] On interpretation, see *Problem of Christianity*, II, lectures XI-XIV, especially pp. 206-221.

made noble efforts, but the best model of community on earth was the community of scientific inquirers:

> If, then, you seek a sign that the universe contains its own interpreter, let the very existence of the sciences, let the existence of the happy inventive power which has made their progress possible, furnish you such a sign. . . . Full of wonder is nature. But the most wonderful of all is man the interpreter,—a part and a member . . . of the world's infinite Community of Interpretation.[40]

Although Peirce had made science not merely the paradigm model but the form of the ideal, Royce wanted to retain a warmer, even commonplace idea of community. An orchestra, for example, interpreting a composer to an audience in a spirit of devotion to the interpretation, was a community. Any organized society whose members acted in the spirit of interpretation was a community. A community was something a man could love as he loved his father or mother or lover, and an unregenerate man could even hate a community. Royce's ideal of community, for all its resemblances to Peirce's, was not nearly so radical. It preserved the individuality of the members and allowed them, even encouraged them, to act out familiar passions. In the end Royce remained nearer to Baldwin than to Peirce. Despite all Royce's concern with infinitude and technical perfection, he did not share Peirce's stark demand for a final choice between ordinary human concerns and the ideal of truth.

Royce's relative similarity to Baldwin became obvious at the outset of World War I. He began at once to speak for the allies, and whatever hesitation he felt about actual intervention was soon resolved. Royce's and Baldwin's reaction to the war revealed the quality of their conservatism. In general intellectuals who were satisfied that Western European and American civilization was basically sound, despite all its many flaws, opted at once for the Allied cause. Doubting progressives—the *New Republic* group, or Dewey, or even Ross—had to endure a period of soul-searching before they could decide that Germany was an intruder on a relatively satisfactory England, France, and America. Only genuine radicals like Randolph Bourne (or probably Peirce, had he lived) diagnosed the war as a symptom of deep social ills suffered by one side as much as another. For his part, Royce decided almost at once that Germany was a culprit, an enemy to

---

[40] *Ibid.*, pp. 417-418, 432.

loyalty and community. He did not relish the war, of course, but he did feel confident that the belligerents were clearly unequal ethically, that the Allies were, in the main, the party of virtue and the Germans the enemies of loyalty and community.[41]

The war had the same pronounced effect on Royce's thought that it had on Hall's and Baldwin's. It forced him to decision and to an effort at working out a program for putting the community ethic into practice. In Royce's case the program was an international "insurance" plan against war, probably suggested in part by Peirce's many references to insurance companies. He interpreted the war as a result of dangerous "dyadic" relations between nations. One nation encountered another without a third entity to create the "triadic" relationship of interpretation and community. So, Royce proposed in considerable detail, the nations should establish an insurance fund against war losses or losses from natural disasters. The fund, administered by a board of scrupulously neutral trustees, would complete an interpretive relationship and transform a mere collective of nations into a community. Aggressors would forfeit their policy rights and the victims of aggression would salvage losses by collecting indemnities. The financial security was clearly secondary in Royce's mind to the activity of interpretation involved. In discovering aggressors and investigating losses the insurance trust would literally interpret one nation or group of nations to another. As the nations accepted the interpretations and acted on them, they would be brought into a community of interpretation. Fantastic as the scheme may have seemed to any diplomat or general who noticed it in 1914 or 1916, it was at least a proposal to begin construction of what Royce called in his final years the Great Community. The Great Community was to be the international community of all communities, saturated by insurance and interpretation, in which all men could live as members of the same body. The Great Community, Royce's last modification of the community ideal, would be a living embodiment of the Pauline charity, which Royce still hoped "never faileth, and outlasts all earthly vicissitudes."[42]

---

[41] "An American Thinker on the War," *The Hibbert Journal*, 14(1915), pp. 37-42;*The Hope of the Great Community* (New York, 1916), pp. 27-28.
[42] *War and Insurance* (New York, 1914), pp. 66ff; *The Hope of the Great Community*, pp. 34, 50, 62ff.

Conclusion

Royce's scheme of insurance against war rings very hollow to anyone coming to it a half-century after the fact, though it could hardly have seemed very practicable even in 1916. The plan for triadic "interpretation" among nations was simply out of touch with the realities of the situation. Royce's end was clear, logical, and had the impressive symmetry that characterized all his notions, but there was no prescription of means, of intermediate steps, of avenues of power that might actually be taken. The test Royce faced was, after all, an extreme one; he was a cosmically-minded idealist trying to come to terms with a reality as disturbing as world war. But his situation was only an exaggeration of the chronic condition of American intellectuals during the period —and since, for that matter. Royce's responding to war with a scheme whose symmetry was matched by its irrelevance was a classic case of the intellectual encountering the apparently unmanageable condition of man in modern, industrial civilization.

The difficulty was not confined to Royce's discussion of war and insurance. The insurance scheme was not any less viable than the absolute or the beloved community, though the futility of the insurance proposal was more obvious. This symptomatic impracticability of Royce's ideals was also a persistent trait of almost all the other intellectual productions of the period. Peirce's community of inquiry was an ideal as perfect and as demanding as any ever conceived, but it was almost perversely impracticable, as though any risk of success would have endangered the consoling power of the ideal. The community of inquiry needed an infinity of space, time, and failure to preserve its compensatory grandeur. James Mark Baldwin's concept of the social man was much more prosaic than the community of inquiry or the beloved

171

community. Still, in practice, Baldwin clearly admitted that in
the United States the quest for moral community had failed. His
moral Atlantis, that ideal compound of American and French
characters, was as artificial and as consolatory as Peirce's or
Royce's ideals of community, and, in Baldwin's case too, what
was missing was a prescription of usable means. The same lack
of a realistic sense of present possibilities permeated G. Stanley
Hall's nostalgia for the virtues of his lost Ashfield and his uncon-
trollable tendency to merely muse about "Mansoul" or the "Bio-
logos." E. A. Ross' nostalgia for the dolichocephalic, "natural"
community of preindustrial America betrayed a similar preoccupation with what was unrealizable.

It was by no means only the subjects of this book who were
trapped by their inability to devise instrumental avenues of at-
tainment to go with their ideals. Most of the other intellectuals
of the period worked within the same brittle cage of ideals of
community that seemed to have no means of concrete realization.
Henry Adams, for example, in *Mont-Saint-Michel and Chartres,*
painted a glorious, semifictional portrait of an age in which social
and religious unity had been the central values and preoccupations. But Adams's historical invention was just as incapable of
realization as anything dreamed by Royce and Peirce. Edward
Bellamy's utopian Boston, in *Looking Backward,* was another
idealized community that had merely sprung into being, not only
without violent revolution but without any significant amount of
human planning, effort, and struggle. It was just as magical in
its own way as Adams' medieval Chartres. A similar case was
Mark Twain's nostalgic recreation of boy life on the Mississippi
or his fond invention of Arthurian England in *A Connecticut
Yankee in King Arthur's Court.* Even so hard-bitten and realistic
a man as William Graham Sumner had his version of a lost, and
therefore unrealizable, community. Sumner often argued that the
United States in the late 18th and early 19th centuries had passed
through the most propitious moment in all human history, a moment that had created a society of genuine liberty and working
equality, but a moment lost beyond recovery.

There were, of course, men who thought they had an eye firmly
fastened on specific means for turning ideals to practice. Henry
George, for example, made something of a career out of what

looked like a practical means, his single tax. Lester Frank Ward's sociology was all aimed at power through the creation of a centralized state—what Ward called a "sociocracy"—that functioned on scientific expertise. But given the actual conditions of the American political economy, neither Ward's sociocracy nor George's single tax had the smallest chance of success. In the last resort their visions were as near to fantasy as Peirce's or Henry Adams'. On the whole, it was a generation in which few men were able to see with any clarity what kinds of enormous new power were being cast up by the industrial process or had any idea how to claim power even if they recognized it, a generation committed to formal dreaming and saddled with futility. Peirce's and Royce's contemporaries did make some enormous strides beyond Emerson's and Melville's. The post-Civil-War generation at least seemed to capture science, and it even attempted to face more directly the realities of industry and the city, no longer turning so often to "Nature," the sea, or some similar metaphor of escape. In general the change was a result of the recognition of society as the inevitable theater in which men's problems and aspirations must be resolved. This kind of recognition of society was clearly the most significant intellectual fact of the postwar decades. It was a long step, however, from recognizing society to creating viable ideals of community, and in attempting this second step intellectuals tended to fall back into eccentricity and failure.

There is a sense, however, in which the social philosophers of the period were responsive to the social and economic realities of the period. The corporation, the Knights of Labor, the Boy Scouts, the Grange, the People's Party, social fraternities and the Ku Klux Klan, the scores of boards of trade and chambers of commerce, the new universities and academic associations, these and a dozen other forms of organization were the most potent new features of American life. The self-determining individual might still be an object of admiration in popular culture, in Horatio Alger stories, and in other forms of success literature. But intellectuals could hardly help recognizing the fact that life in America was becoming increasingly an affair of organization and administration, in which all but the most exceptional individual seemed reduced to impotence and insignificance. The social philosophy of the period recognized—grudgingly, indirectly, and obscurely—what amounted to an organizational revolution, itself unguided and unwanted.

The irony, however, was that organization seemed to destroy community. In the allegorical language of the *Education of Henry Adams,* the superior organization of Boston, with its "premature calculation of tons of coal," broke down the simpler harmonies of his childhood Quincy. Josiah Royce's complaint about the decay of provincial loyalties in the face of a "self-estranged" national organization was only a rephrasing of the same complaint. *A Connecticut Yankee* amounted to an allegorical history of the United States, in which the Yankee used both technology and superior organization to break down the crude but still genuine Arthurian community. John Dewey's more mechanical complaint that there was no longer a real "public" in modern America also hinged on his view that organized technology had undercut old communal habits. E. A. Ross stated the case more explicitly than most of his contemporaries when he deplored the corrosive effect of the new industrial cities on the older natural community of the Middle West. In Bellamy's Boston of the year 2000, for all the superior organization of society, the leading characters did not have a single neighbor or friend. This incipient awareness of the ironic conflict between organizational tendencies and communal habits ran through the writings of most other social theorists of the period. The difficulty they faced was as insoluble as it was simple—there probably *was* no form of community which could be efficient and powerful enough to cope with modern America and still be spiritually bound together by what Peirce called love and Royce loyalty.

Index